CrossWord & Search

100+ Easy Puzzles for Adults. New Format 2 in 1 Crossword and Word Search

+ Free PDF Puzzles

ALL TIME
BRAINSTORM

See all of our books, promotions, and new releases at:

amazon.com/author/brainstorm

Contents

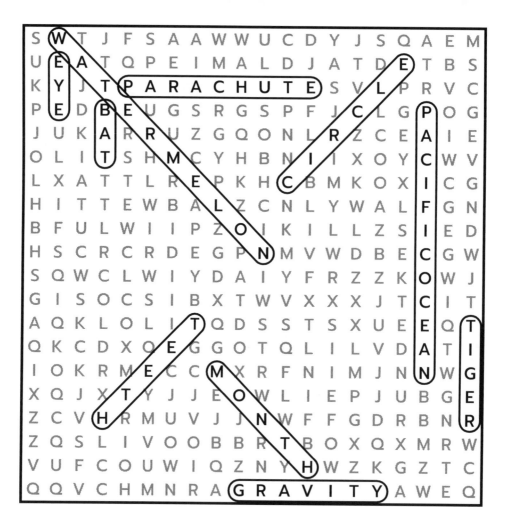

1. What shape does a liquid take when it enters weightlessness? (6)

| C | I | R | C | L | E |

2. What is the largest cat on the planet? (5)

| T | I | G | E | R |

3. What mammal can fly? (3)

| B | A | T |

4. What force causes objects to fall to the ground? (7)

| G | R | A | V | I | T | Y |

5. What is the hardest substance in our body? (5)

| T | E | E | T | H |

6. What is the largest body of water on earth? (12)

| P | A | C | I | F | I | C | O | C | E | A | N |

7. What is the largest berry? (10)

| W | A | T | E | R | M | E | L | O | N |

8. What is a piece of the moon called? (5)

| M | O | N | T | H |

9. What will save a person if he jumps from an airplane? (9)

| P | A | R | A | C | H | U | T | E |

10. Where is the fastest muscle in the body? (3)

| E | Y | E |

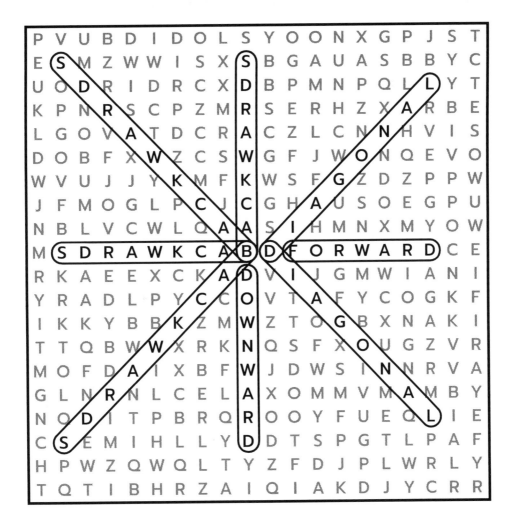

```
R N L J X U Z B E L Q Z S P A G W U H R
J Z E B L C S M I W U D A U U M T Q L Z
Y O Y W Z L K A O Y Y V Z T J X X C H Z
W H R B M K L L C S M T M J D E E P S K
A T A A J M W B K A N K F Q J L R T C E
X V L K Z R P G S W S P U P O F J L Q Y
K R B Y I P E T W T G R A P E G V D K S
A X O D G C E F J V Q K V N K O B R E D
F E N H C R H R I K B Z I D E Q H I T X
F W D Y P C P A N J Z O J R T O Q B Z I
Q E H I F I U S Q S D Z F M I R Q G B E
G Z E F K M B C E P O X U U T G D N M H
R C X C Q H S W W B O P I L A T C I F P
E S P Q M W G J O Q A R F C N Q B M F J
T G M K K L L U E F N F G E I Y J M L X
I E X R R S Q J E A G O D S C K X U K C
X T X C M U R J Z C E S P V E S S H C M
I R E P E S O P E A L W J U P I T E R D
G P U T Z T T X E D F V O F R V E Q U L
M E R G H N V I B E F L C C C Q B B J O
```

answer on page 110

1. Which bird can fly both head first and tail first? (11)

2. What is the name of the work, which is the highest achievement of art? (11)

3. What is the name of the front of the house? (6)

4. Which planet is the largest in the solar system? (7)

5. Which ship sank after hitting an iceberg? (7)

6. What trees grow from acorns? (3)

7. What are the flowers in a bunch called? (7)

8. What is measured by a speedometer? (5)

9. What is the highest waterfall in the world? (5)

10. What are raisins made from? (5)

```
C O N G Z N E E A U H Z C B F N U Z H Z
T L P Z V C L M N B T N T I J B C V D P
D X X Q R R X K P U I O U W K N Y M L D
A N O B O K F G Q T H I R J Z B X A H P
Q T A C T O Q S T Z G Z J R K E A Q Q R
F V Q S A O I A N S W E R H A C H J P C
L Q P O L P E G Z P W C V C I P K K X W
Y D V W U I F B E W U I A T Z K V C S G
C R Z Y C C J I D S W K C T J E L T T V
I M C Q L G Y J D D J R P Z A N U S N O
H U Z Q A J H A X C A B W M Y M A F D A
O X C G C R I F E T B E L T C S A B H T
P R Z J S D N H N L C J G U F M B R Z E
L A T O F S I A M O D A B E E Q F I A M
M S V N M I C V O G X D W D V W Q H O N
W I P Q F X O H H Y G M O U U Q H B S J
T U F N L Y C N J G W K A Y T P I A I F
I V D K F V O I A U A L G O A S X M L N
K L I E V Y A J T O P P R F V I A G S E
R I Y R S W V K W D M W Y A B U E E V S
```

answer on page 110

1. What is chocolate made from? (5)

2. What is the name of a ship with two hulls? (9)

3. What does each question have? (6)

4. What is the name of the device that helps to count numbers? (10)

5. Which star is closest to Earth? (3)

6. What is the largest animal on earth? (9)

7. What is the southernmost continent on earth? (10)

8. What material is every glass in the world made of? (4)

9. In which direction does the sun rise? (4)

10. Which bird imitates human speech? (6)

answer on page 110

```
H K A A C P W E B R T V N S Q N E O M O
C W Q R L Q F P D E P W G S Q E H U M Z
N F W K S R X I U M M L M V X D Q U L D
E Y X P S K W G L O I G J N B S X Z G U
R B J A Y G F E Y T V K E O Q V L R I Z
T N F A L T Z U S E T R A L Q Q B E Q W
A V O M O T O R Z C T O G Y I Y J V X A
N W K L J U Z A V O R F C Z C C R O T Q
A C M L T Z E E A N N U S Y E F O C X T
I S U A T L L G N T W A P S C D D T D X
R W I F C P K C N R U I W A R A R E P I
A M T N X I S S I O L N G R E T Q V A T
M I N I H S I M B L W C R R A P K U T U
G R P A N Q V H O C W P E W M R W D V Y
U P Q R E H O W I F F B E H G S J Y M O
F N M N N E C P E M X W N D D G P P L A
P X Y W S A C G E P B G Z C T Z H O Y E
G O O V S I B A U H F A U C P Z O E Y X
S I F E S Y C H G L I V X T M H T C F X
G Z J C B J U T H A L A R M C L O C K W
```

1. What is the name of the deepest place in the world? (13)

2. What is people's favorite cold sweet treat? (8)

3. What is the heart of a car called? (5)

4. What do people do when they want to remember a moment? (5)

5. Which device can be controlled technics from afar? (13)

6. What wakes a person up in the morning? (10)

7. What is heavy rain called? (8)

8. If not black, then what is tea? (5)

9. What do you put on a blanket? (10)

10. What is put on the pillow? (10)

```
P E L R J F Z O Q T G X D G Y M J L J F
X C Q D X O X M I B T L R K M Y K Y E K
B S M H H Y Z X F R O L Y D A X A U W O
E X A I G M M M T M L Q T K P S E X P B
M R S E N R L O S T E N U O R M B V A E
I U N K X D O Y F H H P U P S K X O K Q
T U R T L E C Q X U A O M E G C B H G C
X W V B E H I G G M A R X A L L N D C D
B L C M S O M K N M N G K C A Y H K R U
S W P K A Z Z V V I S N W O C U G T M P
W O V W I L X T H N Q O T C N P F N P P
M P R S Q Q U R L G A R N K I J V T C A
Y F A E M A O L Q B M N J O C T O P U S
B Q H I C Y R F P I G M D Z Y C E Y L D
G J K J W O J G D R O L T Q S T A C W G
I Z P H Z I N O N D C V I D P R B M F R
K Q F R Q F Z I C M I E B W Z F J J A W
P Q E O X N M X H D U K X N E V A B F X
W O Z B X D L I H R S J C U I E V W X E
X M L T J T N A A F O L I G H T N I N G
```

answer on page 110

1. What do people breathe? (6)

2. What is the name of the arrow in the sky? (9)

3. What do we see on the clock? (4)

4. What is a bird's mouth called? (4)

5. What marine animal has many legs? (7)

6. What is the name of a large predatory fish? (5)

7. Who is slow and has a shell? (6)

8. What is the smallest bird? (11)

9. Who has a horn on his nose? (10)

10. Which bird has the most beautiful tail? (7)

9

```
Q M F H R L Y N V X T A Y O P D Y O J L
L S W Q W X Q Q K F H A Q U P H S A B Z
Z X V F K V C L F R Q M E J U I E B A Z
P W A L T D I S N E Y O S L B V M D U F
W E Q M W P Y Q P B N O V P P T W L P I
M A N J F E M P S M S N G I S D A O R D
T W P G H A D R I V F A M N M C C S F S
I A Q F U R E C R B Q Z V U T G S N C C
M Q O M J I R B X X C X I Z K Q P H T I
M O I X A Y N Z O R P R S S S V H W Q J
N N O Q H Z S J L K A A P G H K Q D Z F
E G S U N D X D U U S X U R E R D B V C
C L E H S K Z F Q Z E L R P T F E E H M
X J T M I I N A B I X G T Q L C N K P E
I S G U M L F Z D E G I A O W Z D O Q F
U N U L E M I P L G P E Y E Y I V D C C
O G Z I L N Q E J R I X L K C K C L X D
O P R K M W M M A J N Z V P V I J Z B Y
Y A A N E G R H H L G Z Q X R Q U E E K
M N X W W M S U K C W Q E S J Q R C V D
```

answer on page 110

1. What is the name of the fish house? (8)

2. What bird can't fly? (7)

3. Who is the most popular green swamp character? (5)

4. What was the name of the princess from The Little Mermaid? (5)

5. What is the most popular cartoon production company? (10)

6. In which cartoon is a squirrel trying to get a nut for a long time? (6)

7. Which statement is not subject to proof? (5)

8. If one angle is obtuse in a triangle, what are the others? (5)

9. What signs do drivers look for on the road? (9)

10. What is hard to do without when traveling? (3)

10

```
F R K B L C Q T D G C E I Q Q S E T B T
M I N T E R N E T U M B D U J R E O L V
C Q B U R Z J B O H D Y A K F D M C S C
O R Q T S D W Q L U K B J A H X B H I G
T M L N Y I B Y R J W Y B W O J A Y H E
C O E H F C V H C H B R E G T M C V N E
A Y D T I K O K C G N I V C P P L O H H
B Z C X J B I F Y H Z H F O H L I K X I
L B D R R M K W F N T F O D E V F H O G
N G E V F X B C C E B V P I T H D Q O A
B F N G H A H T A N E M Q L K V M M D G
R V B R N T V X I P L G G B S M O U B G
Y O D U N G B A T L K U R D K Q W G O I
W D P S C B T Z A D P C M I Z E G G R Q
E G I A V P U A R C R H A U N M L B A U
J C G X A L B N O T J Y Z B T D I L N N
Z F W C U Y R C O Q K P H O G H E D G B
V O B G K M V H T I H I B B W H Z R E F
W K U W M F Z O X N Y C V M X Y P G G A
U W X W U H V R E F R I G E R A T O R G
```

answer on page 110

1. What is the world wide web called? (8)

2. What is the name of the liquid cosmetic hair wash? (7)

3. What color is obtained when red and yellow are combined? (6)

4. What is the name of a household appliance for grinding coffee beans? (13)

5. What is the name of a device for preserving food at a low temperature? (12)

6. Who is in charge on the ship? (7)

7. This boy was raised by animals. What's his name? (6)

8. What is the name of the travel bag? (8)

9. What is frozen water called? (3)

10. If you do not leave it, then the ship will sail away. What's this? (6)

11

```
L Z F B H H Y S C Z Q N O E U H L B C C
O B S X Y X R K R G L T Q I U T N Q F A
W N V D E Q S G S I A P G O Q E A V Z M
Z Z T X L I U B P N E V K S G Q R Q X E
V M P V B A B H Y F O W H C G N W U K L
M P E X U K M B B N B W B X Q R P D A Y
W Z S W Q F A V W I W I Q P R X A L E O
X T Y S X M R P S E U S A H U R Y E J W
T F I M O J I F A K I J N Y J H F U G I
O V J B I D N D Z J S I Y I C Y X F O V
C A C T U S E X C M I O M E M Q M L T R
Z X M K P L B J H J F R L H G A P F Y G
Y V Q E N S H M A E R N K E S Z T K U U
H Q O C U H Z R M A P N Z U Z Q I I T Y
I U Q F S Y O P O K H Z T W F N Y B V F
K K U P E K O S M U A D G S T A F D X J
G F P D X K B L I R C O M P A S S V K C
V P Z I G S N K L L A O F D V J T L D K
J R O O R P R Y E Z O I X S G Q J I G J
K P B M L I A H P B D J N V R V E I E G
```

answer on page 111

1. What nutrients are found in large quantities in fruits and vegetables? (8)

2. What animal is called the ship of the desert? (5)

3. What is the name of a flower with a yellow center and white petals? (9)

4. What is the name of a houseplant with thorns? (6)

5. What usually happens before a rainbow? (4)

6. What falls from the sky in winter? (4)

7. What is the name of the ice peas that fall from the sky? (4)

8. What is the underside of a shoe called? (4)

9. What vehicles do the military use underwater? (9)

10. What device can be used to navigate in any weather? (7)

```
L O M U Z O J S Y L L P N L P Q R H M Z
E W A F X V K K H C U K J U T D C A H A
R I Y G B A D M I N T O N O V A N O B G
R F L E T O R V B C U W T N Z K R W M S
I M L L Z K C S T G J K R K Q A R P Y
U H R X S A G W O Y S T O Y U G I C W C
Q Y Z I H X T P R R Z Z O S E E D H C E
S P N Q Y S R Y Z L A C B Y I J E R M J
V Z Q Z O A G V R R K T C Y H T P I M H
Q A I T B A S W L I X Y I B A K I S C L
C U X X P R I Q B N A K N Y R U K T V E
Y M L K G V Y H U I O F O X R K I M V E
Z N R P I J H O H A B D R R Y K W A M D
L F X T M A P N J P R X T Q P D B S Y Q
Q Q P D V K E T I O U E C C O G D T K P
R E T E M O M R E H T R E N T E Z R R O
F Q N O L M G K E K N L L L T U O E A L
A C R O R R O H U A C M E W E B T E J C
V D P P Y L O Z V U M T B I R T H K V T
F V O W M Y O E O A C Y W H P B Y W M U
```

answer on page 111

1. Which forest dweller dries mushrooms on trees? (8)

2. Which figure has all sides equal? (6)

3. What is the name of the device for measuring body temperature? (11)

4. What is the name of the young wizard who has an owl? (11)

5. What is the name of the sport with racket and shuttlecock? (9)

6. What is the name of the modern online encyclopedia? (9)

7. What is the name of the story where everything is fictional? (9)

8. What is the name of the genre of films that scares the audience? (6)

9. Which tree is the symbol of the New Year? (13)

10. What is the name of a book that does not have paper sheets? (14)

```
Z T A N Z S N N K A Z I G S E C N C T J
A Q J A X K Q S U N S E T V U I Q Z Z O
E B G K Y L E K G P Q L Q H V Z E C N H
U D E V V D Y L M K N Q W T Y R S W R D
M J D P I E B H S Q U D W A P V A P Z P
Z K F A K R S L Z Y Z C B Z I D P B K T
E G N O W U S S A U Q L D U Y Q W E K L
Y T P T A H L D D N D P V B T Z N H Z Y
P X D Q U Y G C V S D Y A K I W B H Z K
V N J K T M I G W S D S V I O J A U I N
I I W N H N B N O E X E C Y N O N G L J
D H N S O P U D L O T V P A R T T O S X
D P B H R E K C U N N Z R U P Z E U W U
B S L R B G R Z M W O J B I K E X R U C
A P A M N I L L N T L H H L M X L D Y I
E S D W C W Z D N P N A S I B U S M F S
C Z E U N Y F Y Z A G M K H X A W N Y K
V X M R B B X Z Z P Z E T R X Q S C G K
S L Z Z G Z Z V K I T T V D U V Z I I H
H U Q N O N V D J G T R B S X N I P Y G
```

answer on page 111

1. What is the name of the school table? (4)

2. What is the name of the phenomenon when the sun sets? (6)

3. What is the name of the phenomenon when the sun rises? (4)

4. What do you get for winning the Olympics? (5)

5. What is the name of the picture of nature? (9)

6. What is the name of the profession of a person who paints pictures? (7)

7. What cats don't have fur? (6)

8. What is the name of the song that each country has? (4)

9. Which geometric figure has no corners? (6)

10. What is the name of the person who wrote the book? (6)

14

```
U Y Y J J N V K Q V Z V H X N S S Y Q F
L K B I A F Y W P N U A J G H T U Z P O
F R C B B Y Y W Z L T S M N I E E F G J
N D R P V Q E M N Y G Y M O N O R T S A
R T H U N D E R S T O R M R X U W Y K A
O O U D O O W Y L L O H S E Y D L Q A I
C C S I I V M K J O F O T B S K A T E S
P S A A O C C O F H U C P Q A X V O T T
O I P K X S U V T B L K M A O I J K F X
P F T M P E U W N N Z E D R W X G D U Z
B M U M F X P O P Z J Y G F P G A Q U A
L F D T P C Z T G F T A D I G H R M X O
F U O M C U B P A K N F Q H D N N R R A
N L W F R R L O B G B N C E K N W Y S O
O L A X D S N I S V O P M C A G X T I U
U M Z E F I T F F D W F X X A T Q C M R
F O Y J E O S U B A O I I N X J U R T G
F O V K P N E R E I U F B N N C R G G O
K N O C Y E O U Z Q R M O T Y M Y T A U
F G U A J W B B D N Y V M H N V Q F W W
```

answer on page 111

1. What can you ride on ice in winter? (6)

2. What is the name of the round moon in the sky? (8)

3. What sports use sticks? (6)

4. What is the name of the guided tour in the museum? (9)

5. What is rain with lightning and thunder called? (12)

6. What natural phenomenon obstructs visibility? (3)

7. What is obtained from corn kernels in the microwave? (7)

8. What is the science of the stars called? (9)

9. Where is the birthplace of cinema? (9)

10. What is the largest musical instrument? (5)

15

```
L L T W Z S Q O H X U A E T M Q O G T A
U D X M A C H S W W I V Y G O L O O Z A
I E B G R P B X L U T J J N J X V M N V
B T H O B Y D Q R P A D L M Y Y N C O T
C V G Z E B K L O K N O D Y T C I I U A
E N I P Z V V G Q P G B Y C P E T Z C R
N W O L C C H A M E L E O N N J K P C C
N Q N N E C K J B O B A L T I F K Q S D
N S R E B B I C R L C Q G O E G K T P W
Y T Z C N J N M C A E R K U U B A J I W
D F P T O H H B F B E V X L M F L M P I
Z S Q A T P U G A E U Y A P Q E Q M W Z
M Q T R Z Z J O C O J C P H Q M J O M X
A D E K L A B E V V Q Y L A G P B S F U
Q Q O R Q A H B O Z C Q X R E S S W Z B
Q O U P B K N C N J T F N B W L B C O F
G I J D O T E A C X Q A F C Q A H T F F
N N G Q G P P R F H H S A J Q W A A C M
H J V J R T B N N U N A H X H N M D V G
G Q B Z I C Y D Z G X S F F Y B G Q I X
```

answer on page 111

1. What animal can change color? (9)

2. What is the name of the striped African horse? (5)

3. What science studies plants and flora? (6)

4. What science studies animals? (7)

5. What is the thickest tree on Earth? (6)

6. Where did the Olympic Games come from? (13)

7. Which tree has a green color all year round? (4)

8. What does a butterfly eat? (6)

9. What is the funniest job in the circus? (5)

10. Which year has more time than any other? (8)

```
W I A H G C Y N V A D D R E S S E E K G
X J Y U F V O E N S J J M Y Q U V M A J
N E L R X B A U D N F L V A V J I A Z N
B R A A F E M I L R H R C A K S I X T N
E A S Q B H C K A C F P O N L Q K Q E E
B O F N O A R N N P L O I F B F W N E E
U S R M X U L M D Y A S K Y M E M C R V
T W A W P W D N Y U W F W Q N Y L Z J B
U P T D L C M X L B F V K K Y N A Q R W
O X S C Q B D C T N P Y O O A K B I D E
Y R R W X Y O G T A C Q X C I J S D D C
N Q A N H A X K Q C C A R L M C Y I L X
Z C L P B N Z M W I O O L G P L A N O D
W Y O X R N J N L B B C P L T P X Y K J
E H P X X P Q K H A K H K G E E G Z M K
L F X N A F U O T R A I Y F W P N N I E
K Q N M V A E Z C A E N N Z B B P Z X C
L L P F B T O K S O P A Q P D J E A Y H
J K H G F A G G H E M T Y H V J P N C D
B H P H Y S I C A L E D U C A T I O N A
```

answer on page 111

1. What school subject is used to test physical strength? (17)

2. What in the sea is a reference point for a sailor? (9)

3. Which country has the highest life expectancy? (5)

4. What is the name of the most viewed video hosting on the Internet? (7)

5. What is the style of unaccompanied singing called? (9)

6. What is the name of one of the most common varieties of coffee? (7)

7. What are vinegar and lemon juice? (5)

8. What is the name of the top of the mountain? (4)

9. What is a circus athlete called? (7)

10. What is the name of the recipient of the letter? (9)

17

```
F G F A D V E N T U R E V Z M S F A X J
B N P H H Q L I E V S Q F O T R C I J N
Z L A S R P T W N L L S X G Z A L M O N
I W W L Y Q E S N Q I N R F W U D H V R
J E V I F V P V I O A E M H D E T K H U
W L T M X D T I S F F P O B E A V C G T
J O H D F L Z Y X K R G R R R B O W K M
C Y A H L Q Y J M D I E M A I M E T L B
L D S B C F V D V A C E M T F G O A D H
Q B W B O O T R S I A A D S A O Z E N W
W C S B I N A U N J J A H S C Z O X R G
P S I H T A V E X O G X F B Q K C N Y S
Y G V B E C C G S E O U P M Z T A I W T
J W Y J U L U C T T U N G I Z Q V L X W
D N U J G O S N G A H H R X N D Q A B R
I N O T H V L K B Y M E L E S H I N B O
E R Z B A L Z Y B F W K T Z T S X E E Y
Z W T B R B L C T U J Z J I A F Q R W W
I A W U H H V Y N Q P N Q W C X A D G L
Z I G W A Q F S W L X M R F X S P A B V
```

answer on page 112

1. What hormone is produced during extreme sports? (9)

2. What is the name of exciting experience? (9)

3. What is the perception of art and beauty called? (10)

4. What is the name of the continent with the world's largest waterfall? (6)

5. What is the daytime called? (9)

6. Which is the most populous continent? (4)

7. What do we call a mountain which could erupt? (7)

8. Which sport is played at Wimbledon? (6)

9. How many rings are there in the Olympic Games symbol? (4)

10. What is the longest running race in the Olympic Games? (8)

```
O M H J C G H F B H S C M E V N U F Q R
P U X K T S Q B O J R Y Z F G B Y W F X
V Y K E R G H U O H E G P O Q S I W L Z
A Y P K E S C C I V H O M T L P H N N T
A H V A H W V P X A K L D Y N Q P Y I I
Y A E U S S E S S Y Q O B D E E V Q E R
L G A Q R L Y H Z W G H M N N G O E T N
M R M H X A N A B I S T W K K F R A S E
Z E A T E P N K Y U B I V S C P O J N E
Y E Z R Q L Q I F H N N C F J U S Z I W
T N D A V B I S U J T R K A H P B G E O
E L H E P T J N A M K O G J Y H J T T L
V A L S E A D K Y D S X Z E P D A H R L
W N G U I Y A D N U S K B Y X Z M G E A
N D N J U L V Z C G A C Q T L K T L B H
M J J E N R G W H G Q Y C A S X I A L O
Z S B E N H O N L V Q K M P N Z G L A Q
Z K C A H M L T E B I K S E A W A W O C
E H C G H I P W M W E F V R I C Q S N K
Z F W W F V V O N H M C B M J T Y V T V
```

answer on page 112

1. Who developed the theory of relativity? (14)

2. What do we call the study of birds? (11)

3. What natural phenomena are measured by Richter scale? (10)

4. Which is the most spoken language? (7)

5. Which is the heaviest natural element? (7)

6. Which country produces the most coffee in the world? (6)

7. What is the first day in English calendar? (6)

8. What holiday has a symbol as the pumpkin? (9)

9. What is the world's biggest island? (9)

10. What is the world's longest river? (4)

19

```
K E A N U R E E V E S B V N O U A N C L
B V P G P S O Y S T E R S E B E V R C P
S T M Y N G E O S H I S L W Q Y B U V X
E F V Q T O J A E T K C S Y D I Q B Y T
K G J G D L S X Y W T J G O F F N P E F
H A A K I H K S X Z L H R J D Z E F V
K X V B A Y F C C F K I K K M J U H G V
Y A R O B C J F J A L U R S Y J O E W H
N X Z Z K A O Y B P J I K R P T A N V E
M I L N H O B V B Z R R A Y N Y U I O J
J V V M E T B S G S C I E M M H R R Y J
E B I W K B W V E Z U F T T T I K A M D
K Y Z W Q E L P B L R V A D E O Y H R H
W O S A A Z U R D H R G N M P P H T D U
R V W T A O C E A O P A J E K M A A X U
A P H U B A J L C K Y H H Y U N Q K A I
C E V F N U G P T J V O B C D T U R O O
R D O W Z A I E I H G J V Q Z L R Y K I
V L H V C F D S J X K F I I J Q Y O W E
V Q X X I K R N J F Y S F C T Y Z N N Z
```

answer on page 112

1. Who directed the Lord of the Rings trilogy? (12)

2. Which actress has won the most Oscars? (16)

3. Who played Neo in The Matrix? (11)

4. Who is often called the father of the computer? (14)

5. Which email service is owned by Microsoft? (7)

6. What part of the atom has no electric charge? (7)

7. What is meteorology the study of? (7)

8. What animals are pearls found in? (7)

9. In which US city is Broadway located? (7)

10. Who is often credited with creating the world's first car? (8)

```
I F L C G E J G P T N H H D A E K P E S
E Z A O W I A P V O I O J S E N U R P Z
C K E R N X Y C M V Y R L X T P H R X Z
V I M J O H Y H A X Z S M U R U G U A Y
T A G L Z C L I H B S E C X X Q A U N D
D L W W J T A N J V H X W O F V K H I E
Z Z W S V I T A M X V M G R M S E W E Z
U U T X Q A I A R G N G R F P A H M O D
A L L E A P Z N P J R J X U R R I D Q Z
L R P I I D K U F A T W L T M L Q Z F X
W R B S Y C X F C U X Y C H G C A Z E K
R N V D R N Q B C G H B F I N Y F C N T
M F M P N V A Q Q H Z Y G B I L H F U L
H W S D Y L O M S T Q Q B Q M Y N Z Z C
J W F M Q Q J E R I A B E C F O U Q F T
L Y H V L M O B R E B F A L H N H U M J
P N L C O N A Z A G G T F X C Y O U T U
F I B N Z E H W I F O B T X B C F K P F
I C H I C K P E A S T W Y P A K S Q M G
Z Z B R B N J C B I A G E B S U M Y D L
```

answer on page 112

1. Which animal can be seen on the Porsche logo? (5)

2. What country won the very first FIFA World Cup? (7)

3. What other name does "corn" go by? (5)

4. What is the common name for dried plums? (6)

5. What's the primary ingredient in hummus? (9)

6. Which country invented tea? (5)

7. What is the national dish of Spain? (6)

8. Which European nation was said to invent hot dogs? (7)

9. Which country is responsible for giving us pizza and pasta? (5)

10. Which organ has four chambers? (5)

```
R M A F R C W V O T T S E S S N S D Q N
D M K I A K V N W Q H Y Q H C J Z D C X
B D S B M E Q R T E Q L M O T S F U R K
Y W W M L Y P B G S W N H A J C C J D Q
A S P C P L T Z D F K N Q R A A R F P N
N D T D Y C V J K X V P Z A T M X F I I
N X X I N Z Z X J S F U K H U A G S U X
I T U A Q S O T L W J C O P N R F F A T
C R T L C S A H A R A L F I J S S M R O
D O R A M W W T M L I S K I N X P S T K
O S K S L X H J O C C N S F V D D H A U
V G S K V C K L I D K E U Q O G O T P Y
E K A A J D A S L D K J N X W B L T O Y
P H J J K G M L W L W T U A C T A Y E D
H R K Y U R G P C K W W W I C X F R L M
S N O R U E N M R I J B F T X I O P C B
A R J V J O C Y R O U I O Q R A T W F Y
L X M Q Y X S D T D F M Y A Z U L A X O
C O B Q P Y R A M I D S O F G I Z A V F
L E Z J D B S D K W Q F W Y B C M Z V K
```

answer on page 112

1. What is your body's largest organ? (4)

2. What kind of cells are found in the brain? (7)

3. Which element is said to keep bones strong? (7)

4. Which American state is the largest? (6)

5. What is the smallest country in the world? (7)

6. Which of the Seven Wonders is located in Egypt? (14)

7. Which desert is the largest in the world? (6)

8. By what name were the Egyptian kings known? (8)

9. Who which queen was Julius Caesar involved with? (9)

10. Which religion dominated the Middle Ages? (11)

22

```
O X F Z Z R J U I L C W M S U Y X E S Z
K Z F T W I Z Y N I Q R T C S H C K S L
B L E A L A O K P T E H Q B S G Z P E P
T G E Y H L G N I C A R E S R O H U D N
X Q W D Y S Y L G A B J M E S Q F R B S
Y B R M H K K R J H O J K Y S B A I V C
O X P M Y Y Z H K L R Z S W A U M X I P
O U G Z F L X O V K Q J U F P S F J T G
S T H A N K S G I V I N G D A Y Q K G K
N I B B K A P D O I C W U S X E O T L A
U I E J R X X D V E F K P A F T N F Z U
T F O S O R C I M P Y S B F F U O R B R
E W Z K T L Z C U Z T D A D C O Y V R F
D C T A J M P Q Z D O R D V T W O B U Y
A R J A U G R W G O I R D B B B J P M D
X L Z R Q R G Z H G O O A R F F I I U J
E Z Y D M E X Q H O I L A X L J W L X R
L X A T K U I J I K L F F J B T D X N L
O N L R E P N M Y C Y N K B P W B V U O
R O C H E E T A H D M Y F X A C V I G P
```

answer on page 112

1. What is the name of the home of the Greek Gods? (7)

2. Which mammal has no vocal cords? (7)

3. What's the fastest land animal in the world? (7)

4. Bill Gates is the founder of which company? (9)

5. Which watch company has a pointed crown as its logo? (5)

6. What sport is featured in the video game "FIFA"? (8)

7. What holiday is called "turkey day"? (15)

8. Which Australian animal enjoys eating eucalyptus leaves? (5)

9. What was Louis Armstrong's chosen form of music? (4)

10. What takes place in Hong Kong's Happy Valley? (11)

23

```
I K Y I K V L X J H P K Y F E K H S J J
L A Q N K I N Q M F V L V Z L F I R I X
C Z P S X Q Z Q H H G N X U W J N L C V
O H C T Q R S C X O O O M X R K R J Z F
D A B D B L X A M G N B O C D C B C L V
O A H S E Y B Q A U P G B E C P E P I H
N T N N Z S J T Y T A F K T J A C O Y B
C A V C D E N T L Z X B P O T O B V F G
T T E X Z E V F I A X R C J N X A H Q Y
W N R C P K N U C W E W D H J G P G N I
U Q K I O O S D I L A O P T N M Q S Q L
M S T X D N I A S I H B N N Y C T S S F
F T E N D E A W N I B T A W H Y T K C D
P Z O V Z S J I Z J Z B D K V Q S O K E
S L P S E W F U D F L P Q B X G M R X D
D C L T P N W X T N R P E C B R L W Y O
M X U O R A H G X Z I I A W H Q J L N Q
A L T N K I I P Z C I L K N A U F K L U
I H O U F U J N C V M H V N D H I R O Q
P E W X V V L H O N O L U L U A K P K Q
```

answer on page 113

1. Which country does the sport of pelato come from? (5)

2. Which ocean surrounds the Maldives? (11)

3. Which planet shares its name with a dog? (5)

4. What is the world s largest office building? (8)

5. Where was built the first subway? (6)

6. What is the national animal of China? (5)

7. What is the noisiest city in the world? (8)

8. How many continents are there? (5)

9. On which Italian island is Palermo? (6)

10. What is the capital of the American state Hawaii? (8)

24

CrossWord & Search

#20

```
S U L K F U S M Z H U Y S O I T Z B M C
P S R V L M D B X V I J R O R F C B Z M
O Q C V T E N B W R E K O T S M A R B G
N S A T B C O O F D Q P S B X Y B A S S
D A N X G Z R N L N F W V H A R J B A B
A K A T J N Q D A E E J U Z R K X H Q N
G A D W V R U F C R G Z Z W X J U Z Q X
U T A N R N A B P N D N G P G I X N Z A
E T O B Q H I P F D R O A M A H H F F O
R N B R E W B S X T E O D L O Y R S A M
R V P F O B O G B F V J C A E T E R L T
E D G W E N D S Z C S D J I V H E Z K X
K Z I J I X T D O M R X M H N I C A M P
A C O D F W C O L Z T Y I F O U N I U E
A C X K W T Y N U E Z J P S I O F C M F
B L E Q V M T G T B R T S O V W N R I K
A O P N Q M Y Q O O Y A I R E O P U P B
Z H B A H C Y A D Q C E M U B D I W E X
Q Y J P F E Y S X I F B O H K Z H L X R
T I C Z D K O O P F V F P G R E E C E G
```

answer on page 113

1. What is the largest city in Canada? (7)

2. What is Scotlands National Animal? (7)

3. What is the lowest male voice? (4)

4. Which country does Celine Dion come from? (6)

5. Who was the original author of Dracula? (10)

6. Who is the inventor of photography? (8)

7. Who did the Mona Lisa paint? (15)

8. Who painted the ceiling of the Sistine Chapel? (12)

9. In which country was the famous painter El Greco born? (6)

10. Who did paint the famous painting Guernica? (7)

25

CrossWord & Search

#21

```
C F C U M U R S V M B H B I X I B X H P
G K S D B V O E N I M W F I S E Q S X Z
P N R T D U R Z G E G E L G R O F W I X
E Y Y M N O H O W L L Y K W C Y L M X A
Q Z T G N B A N Q D L L X S L F C I O N
X O V A N U D I S L I E A T T K H S A T
C R Z C Q Y X T N I B S M Y X F T C B O
B U N I A P S N I V T M R M D B F Y G N
D F U J Y E U A B K H A V T F O B Z A I
F U M J A V B R S N B I L T S G O L O O
L H W M R G F A O L R L D F J T R W B S
U Z A K C Y U T L L O L D E L E V E N A
Z N G D X C J N J A B I Z O V P K Y U L
P C O B K I J I C C B W L Z I H G L Q I
R C H G J X H T J P O N T M W A M B N E
P V Q B E K Z N I Q W I G S E X J U X R
W M P P Q F Q E D G M B S L I A K R K I
Y W L X W T B U X K A O U T V X A X L U
T V U X Z W S Q K L N R B H L Y Z J U O
U U K Z P K U G M N O I P M A C E N A J
```

answer on page 113

1. In which city did Romeo and Julia live? (6)

2. How many oscars did the Titanic movie got? (6)

3. What is the pseudonym of Allen Stewart Koningsberg? (10)

4. Who is the director of Reservoir Dogs? (16)

5. Who is the director of the X-files? (9)

6. Who did play the role of Peter Pan in the Peter Pan movie? (13)

7. Which country is the largest producer of olive oil? (5)

8. What is the profession of Popeye? (6)

9. Who was the director of the movie The Piano? (11)

10. Who was Mozart's big rival in Amadeus? (14)

```
M K K U W G Q Q A K T U J P R G R S Q T
A G A C B D M U V Q L Y Z A O D D S H F
D K M K F F R P W D X C Q K I Q A D K J
R H B O Y E Y T T U Y A R K B R P F O L
E N F E X R A N B H X M A O E K O S T X
T L O Y M U D E D V C P P D E U E X R C
S H H T I Q L V V M T Z N Q O P O G X L
M C N K G F K K Y L H A Q R H M N X R X
A O Y W A N E X B R B I L I T D I H M R
W U M S T Q I R W O F V N X I Z C V P M
E N T Q K Y B H I H Z E H M T V A K O O
N T E Z S D N N S K L G M E O Q P I J B
J Z O P F D O I F A D U Q Q X Z L O M F
N E Z E E T R Q D W W E U V F L A F T O
B P B K N M J A Q U W E R C O R S I C A
H P U A P F K G P D A Q G O I W U D Q T
B E A X S P W J A A T J E R D M Z G O Y
U L B C G G C G S F Z F I A O E E S G H
O I X S G E F F I L C D A R L E I N A D
R N A X B D H P I A Q O X R S M G Y K V
```

answer on page 113

1. Who played the lead role in the movie Scarface? (8)

2. Who played Che Guevara in the movie "Evita"? (15)

3. Who played Harry Potter in the Harry Potter movie? (15)

4. Which German Count invented the zeppelin? (13)

5. Who was the first president of the USA? (16)

6. In which city was the Titanic built? (7)

7. What was the name of Napoleon's first wife? (9)

8. On which island was Napoleon born? (7)

9. Who discovered Greenland? (10)

10. What was the former name of New York? (12)

```
R  Q  I  L  V  Y  Y  C  M  I  X  C  J  O  R  N  E  N  I  I
B  O  T  M  Q  B  K  R  S  N  L  T  D  V  B  H  I  R  Z  U
C  C  T  N  E  S  I  W  B  E  I  T  Q  P  X  V  Y  M  B  F
P  S  P  U  Y  X  R  L  E  S  Z  Z  M  W  D  T  K  J  B  G
A  Y  D  S  S  W  N  K  P  P  E  K  I  N  G  E  S  E  H  C
L  S  A  D  V  O  H  T  Y  O  P  V  C  R  Z  K  R  S  N  A
E  K  E  Z  D  F  E  H  X  Q  B  M  C  W  B  C  I  N  X  L
O  U  V  O  M  M  L  S  T  G  A  D  Z  C  C  V  L  R  O  O
N  S  R  P  T  U  Y  D  F  N  K  H  X  D  P  L  A  S  Q  C
T  S  S  X  F  I  Y  R  N  Y  N  E  I  Q  P  N  N  Z  M  I
O  S  G  T  C  C  U  E  U  C  M  X  I  E  C  B  K  A  B  V
L  Y  V  O  S  V  I  Q  S  V  H  Q  D  D  H  L  A  N  F  B
O  P  P  E  D  V  T  X  S  X  L  G  R  F  E  W  B  T  I  G
G  K  O  Z  D  J  Z  Q  O  O  B  I  Y  L  C  T  B  S  Z  Q
Y  G  B  E  T  V  O  U  C  N  M  U  P  J  W  M  N  I  Q  B
P  K  T  Y  X  D  C  N  J  K  H  A  W  X  R  X  C  C  X  H
V  X  I  M  T  G  R  K  W  Z  M  K  P  L  A  N  K  T  O  N
Q  C  F  B  J  P  T  H  N  S  U  U  K  X  P  H  X  J  Q  H
I  F  C  K  N  C  L  Y  K  D  X  X  Z  V  S  G  C  D  U  G
W  M  U  J  Q  E  D  B  H  T  E  I  I  M  Q  V  L  K  D  S
```

answer on page 113

1. Which country was formerly called Ceylon? (8)

2. Which dog used to be sacred in China? (9)

3. What is the study of fossils called? (12)

4. What do dragonflies prefer to eat? (10)

5. What is the name of the European Bison? (6)

6. What is called a fish with a snake-like body? (3)

7. In which city is the oldest zoo in the world? (6)

8. After which animals are the Canary Islands named? (4)

9. Which plant does the Canadian flag contain? (5)

10. What is the food of penguins? (8)

```
W I W K H I N L Y P M S K K C H P F R S
J U O I F O T H V P Y A H B H Q W V Z H
A O Y R O P P C B Y B R B O I O S Y B T
K F E C E E R G I U O Q S G H U I B K S
O D C W H Y J M C W O H I L U L E X B S
U A I G H B Y D T R I T X S A B A W T G
R W R R D R U B S R X J H Y H Z I L D L
T P E S Y D N E Y M S X J Z U Y A P P J
B Z G U D V X P T K M M S D A L N L L D
E P I E N U F H C S B Y Y L M N O L R D
U G T K P U V B Z X J U X O O U J Y S E
C N N G Z I V T V E N D N G T S M X E W
A B A L T W X C M T U D K W C O Z T J C
L L I T P L Q E P X S U L Y P A N P L Y
Y X R D R M P A K P L G Q B E I Y V I A
P S E O R Q L O T N A H P E L E K E V J
T J B O J F T U Y G W O B B N W Q R S T
U Z I K O R L I Y T J M L X Q D T X W H
S M S L M G C Z D E J G O V S A O I S W
W C I N C I P K T M E X V V C Q S W H A
```

answer on page 113

1. Which is the largest species of the tiger? (13)

2. Which mammal cannot jump? (8)

3. Which animal wash their food before eating? (7)

4. Which is the smallest breed of dogs? (9)

5. What is the name of an evergreen tree growing in Australia? (10)

6. What is the largest city in Australia? (6)

7. Which nuts are used in marzipan? (7)

8. From which country does pitta bread originate? (6)

9. Which country is the origin of the cocktail Mojito? (4)

10. What is called a meal in open air? (6)

29

```
Z U P R S V N B B Q N E V Y R P U C M J
H X A T I Q X J W V N T F J B D R T U W
Q I P A V A O Z Q G J H K A A V N B H X
S I R C H G S A W O H H K R P L E C R E
L S I O Z D J B B H Q O W E B H V Q J P
S F K A L L E R A Z Z O M D E X M X S E
V A A Y P M G Y T I B R K N D V Q D U C
B F U K G K D S Q R Q Q U A I V E X I I
P C R L K D A C C M E S V I X E L G Y R
B D R K R B S S C V W C U R O G R O N I
R A R E O S H N N I X Z V O I K X Z E X
G F T E K P G F T A T M M C D L R Q I V
Y A H S I B N Z O G X N R L N W M P W A
W O L S R V E J K Z D V D M O K D C X W
R G A X T R I V J C Y S P V B V U I X X
W N B K L C P F A V J I J J R O G X L P
G S I A I E E Q T E R J O B A Y W U R P
G T N T T W T Y B O R P Y M C G Z Z I P
P D C R L A I N R A W A D D T X S C Z D
E V A G A T L Y Z O X F T K Y A O Z G E
```

answer on page 114

1. Which cheese is traditionally used for pizzas? (10)

2. What is the name of the gas that let rise bread dough? (13)

3. What is Japanese sake made from? (4)

4. What is bottled a lot in the French town Vichy? (5)

5. What is the Hungarian word for pepper? (7)

6. What is a banana called in Malaysia? (6)

7. What is the only ingredient that is not found anywhere except India ? (9)

8. Which fruit is also an animal? (4)

9. From which cactus is tequila made? (5)

10. From which country is the famous Emmental Cheese? (11)

```
T N M O E Z I E W U S O X E K Y F H H R
S O P E P R Y L Z S D Z S J E M O W F Z
K G W H K F Z I O L W I X Q F K H S U U
Y A C M V Z L D H D X A J W Q L W S U A
F R L S B Y Z O W H H P B S I U Y X Q Z
O D E U L B M C U J E V E C T F S F T A
M O V B C Y U O Z V C Q H N Y R I H I P
U D D R I E M R T L U I H J G S L V Q C
C O I T Q V E C P O U B C P C U K R A N
K M J X J G H Y I U R C Q Q D R I D P A
E O O W O U T A D D L H A K U J P N E M
S K N T A Q N B T P U O X N Q U W Z S C
U W B I E J A A S D I O Y V A Z T S X P
O S P J Z N S E W P E P G S Z C D E C U
H P J D U Z Y K E H C A A E K S O U R I
E J X X U N R B Z I Y G J P Y P R N J C
T N D G Y T H Q Z Y Z V C C P E K E D N
I F A Y J K C F X B M F Z I X P F T M A
H S K Q X L T H R W Z Z C X I W K E D L
W U T Q U W E T K R S O C N P I P I G J
```

answer on page 114

1. Which French town is known for its mustard? (5)

2. What is the most spoken language in Belgium? (5)

3. In which house does the American president live? (10)

4. What flower is the symbol of the sun and the symbol of Japan? (13)

5. What color is mollusk blood? (4)

6. Which birds have scales on their wings? (8)

7. Which animal has green-colored fat? (9)

8. What is the largest snake on earth? (8)

9. What is the largest tree in the world? (7)

10. What is the largest lizard in the world? (12)

31

```
S R A Q F D O N B I C X V N Z Q N F K W
N Z K B T T Q M E O V V O E G G I B O S
M R W Y A S N A H U O F T H O S K I X T
R V H M I Z N N O B W Z D R Z M P N R S
P P O W Z O D G U P E F I N W W M G Z Y
V T J E I V Z O P J S L F F P S U N E Q
F P Q N A J W W K I L Q Z D I R P O S B
S Z O X D R P O L A W Z Y V O F O T G R
H U Z T U X D U D A T X F J O L P J T G
X K K Q P P G I P D E C V G E S W U H I
O I J R B J W F X P W Z K H C S S D A P
E P O L A R B E A R C Z X K A X A H M O
Z F Q R L Y O P C X O D R I Y H I B E I
R E J U Q O G D F H N L Q A U X K C R Z
G X B E A I H M N T D M L F C O N J I Y
F M P G V S L X F J O N A M A I Z B C T
P E M Z D D T B L R R R A R R R I E A W
X W T Y G F V I T F Y Z R F A W W I J T
P Q K L V A B U W O J X X A M Q A M T U
V H W Z R A T T F G O L X A C O C H R W
```

answer on page 114

1. What is the largest predator in the world? (9)

2. What is the largest great ape? (7)

3. Which vegetable is used to make ketchup? (6)

4. What is the largest vegetable? (7)

5. What is another name for passion fruit? (8)

6. Where did tomatoes originate from? (7)

7. What is the rarest bird on Earth? (6)

8. What is the name of a vegetable that is rich in vitamin A? (6)

9. Which vegetable makes your eyes tear when you peel it? (5)

10. Which fruit tree is considered to be sacred in India? (5)

```
G D Y G L S O C D G D A U I G B L P T O
H H C D W G Q N M S X J I R E S A D E V
P H L S Q P Y Y O X P Q B G A D H F F J
L C E N T R A L A S I A R A W R R A O N
G Q H W M V H K I P C O E N L Z P C L X
T V I X L Q Q N E P X G A W S Q G V W Q
X B K C A G U T I H P B D F X Q K U L B
S F S D N R W I F A C Y Q C A K J P N U
U M W W Y I E T Z X T T M N X E Q E V V
P T T E E M V P I B D I I M P C R Y I O
D J G L J E N A O K I G R W E Y Q U A D
Z Z D I Z U T U D L R I Z B E Q F F B P
L S J V W B O H C O N N J G T T L V I M
S V E W Z H I M E P D W F P Y A I N X Z
B Q B M V F Q X M A C R E U O Y E H Y U
S J C I U K P K U M R B A G G V F R W T
E S B Y A G H M J C T T N N C A C X G G
I V K C L W E A E Q T A V I O B N M L V
V W J I R X R L Z L F V Z P O E R A T L
E S O W S F V D B D H Y B U V L L P G G
```

answer on page 114

1. What plants are often called to as "alternative meat"? (7)

2. What is the largest butterfly in the world? (10)

3. What is the most famous building in Sydney? (5)

4. What is the real meaning of the Greek word Pita? (5)

5. Which region produces the most apples? (11)

6. What is the name of a medicinal mud? (5)

7. What do you call a motorcycle with four wheels? (4)

8. What is the meaning of the Arab word Habibi? (10)

9. Who painted the Mona Lisa? (15)

10. Australia used to be a dominion of which country? (12)

33

```
N V L H X O B W N A S S V S B K V N N Q
O Q H G M W R F H C P M K T U Z S Q K S
T X Z E S Z I O G T D X M L O Q E S Q B
G Z C N Z U L K B F F B W N G S I U W B
N M S X O A E U C R Z Y S F J P F Y H Q
I X X T O Q T P E H L B M N T B Z X R K
H R K P T L L S J U T K O P S K G A E L
S S K X O J C J Q Y W U P F U N Z Z E C
A F S H H O O C P Y G R B W T O V K N V
W U G J E B J H P P K A B J P X H E C F
E V M T D T U E Z D Y D L O Y Q F D B O
G U T Z O B P E S N O V C D L O L F D G
R B S E D C Z S J L J S N C A M Z S N G
O C A J G D P E H T T A V L C V V K A V
E Q G M R N D X U E D A C E U A M G U B
G B A Z W Z E J Q A V E C I E O A S A A
V B K T M P C D M M Y H R R T R B B Z G
N T K C M Y D A L G Q Q L Z I L E L K S
H G B A E Q R X R A Z I Z N X K E F U U
H I L E C E M I H H D O I C V D X C V E
```

answer on page 114

1. What kind of food is Manchego from Spain? (6)

2. Which American president appears on a one dollar bill? (16)

3. What is the tallest tree in the world? (10)

4. What is another word for wall painting or mural? (6)

5. Which language group includes Irish, Welsh and Breton? (6)

6. What is the islamic term for fast? (7)

7. What is the Turkish word for lamb? (5)

8. What word is used in Hawaii both to greet and to say goodbye? (5)

9. Who was the first man to fly around the earth with a spaceship? (7)

10. What color is cobalt? (4)

CrossWord & Search

#30

```
Q P Q W X Q E K T Y P E W R I T E R B Z
A N R O A Z A E G W D P F E Q R G R C Y
X Q O J F W L C I H P T P A X N D B C F
J F B O Y K E L M V K O N I D H C H P Q
G A E T F I D H P W C B A B O S R A J D
C M R T X A N Y O S E U C S D P W L A M
A X T P Y H A D E F F P N U N S M A M L
C D O V W D C L T R A K H H F U G N E B
H D P V A K E Y L G H W B W I S O S S P
I I P E K T N P T W G H P N B L X H W T
F B E G Q T V K B O U H I L O Z K E A O
L J N K O A N U R S R M U S M B P P T P
L M H U B Y G N K S U R Q Y A W R A T I
B P E Y B I N J D L K Q I R S B B R C A
B L I E G Q A U A T T D O C C G I D N R
F D M M O V T A O T Y M G U E U R R A Y
F C E M Z V V P G M E J M M U L S T K X
N O R H S S K E H T I A F A B A L K K T
W O K Z G U F W E O I Q W T Q A N I F E
Z Q Q T P C A R P U Y C J T J F A J S G
```

answer on page 114

1. Which device do we use to look at the stars? (9)

2. Which unit indicates the light intensity? (7)

3. Who is the father of the atomic bomb? (17)

4. Who invented the barometer? (10)

5. Who was the first American in space? (11)

6. What is the name for sculpting hedges? (7)

7. What is the lightest existing metal? (9)

8. Which device was invented by Henry Mill? (10)

9. Which device is used to measure the air pressure? (9)

10. Who was the inventor of the steam engine? (9)

35

```
T N J Y Z V Z S G R D A G Z W Y C G H N
D E D X R W Z V Z I G F Y I I D B W R A
J G P U T O N H W D A O F H J W M O J N
D N E H S C S E N Q C Z J X N T K L X X
E K A K A R X E I B M T T I M Q T N S X
J B R L U N G L L B N K D N O M A I D
Z Z M K E O H F O I A C R E L B B C R L
N N J J R X V Z W X T R I C K A B L I A
G D X D S X A S G R O P M V U G U S U G
J L Y J W N X N N E K J E S Q W D J S H
N H F I F T R B D O R N D R T I H Q S D
Y E T U J T L E F E L S W U O R L L H T
Z Z T K A Q N P O F R G D R F S O L J G
P B M M D P S M Y P N F E X J G F N Y L
Z B R F U X C R F H D T L C N S M F G D
M V A O G O U A F D S Y J E H I V S R L
R S V K O C O K F A V E L M M C Z M Q P
G N I M R A W L A B O L G M K I J L Y B
O A X E T O U R J U R A S S I C N U C U
O O M Z M P V Q S E V N K V O V W G Z O
```

answer on page 115

1. Who discoved one of the first antibiotics: "penicillin"? (16)

2. Which planet is nearest the sun? (7)

3. Which natural substance is the hardest? (7)

4. What is the lightest chemical element? (8)

5. What is the brightest star in the northern hemisphere? (6)

6. In astronomy, what are Pallas, Vesta and Davida? (9)

7. Who was the first person to step on the moon? (13)

8. Birds and mammals evolved from which group of animals? (8)

9. During which period did dinosaurs live? (8)

10. What is a long-term increase in the Earth's average temperature called? (13)

```
T A R W S P N S H F S R S T O O P S D A
A J L V Q A B H J Z B G E H E O X Z Z P
Q K F E H I M B C P K P H S G G C S U L
X Q A G Y F J V D H N U C U C M I M N C
M F D S E P M W V B I F B Q G R Q W J A
O L L R P N K Y I Y P C M E A C L Z G V
I M H E B C O Y M N L M X R S N U Y J M
O S A X X H I F W D O E R U N M C H R C
Q H Q B L Z Z O D U G E G C R C B F M D
O M S P M R L H Z B F R T K F A R Y X O
N K P Z O Q X F V O A Q X G S D N O Z N
V I U G S Y T G Z H S C K Z Q I F C Y A
P G I J H T Z N P Y C E S J G L W N U L
E N E S T X E S Q E X A M S Q L M X I D
Q O O I U Y D F I F T Y X T F A R B S S
H I W H I P L X J K L U Y K F C P K E Q
Z L H T Y R W Q R F O I R O G M Z G G A
S J X Z F R S O R B O N N E M E M O N B
V E M A K X H S I G M K E Z W U T V A I
L G E L D R Z D T A V E U X T Q C Q G V
```

answer on page 115

1. How many stars has the American flag got? (5)

2. Who invented Ferrari? (11)

3. What is the most famous university of Paris? (8)

4. Which animal is on the golden Flemish flag? (4)

5. What is the name of the Indian holy river? (6)

6. What colour to do you get when you mix red and white? (4)

7. What is both a French wine region and a luxury American automobile? (8)

8. Who is the largest toy distributor in the world ? (9)

9. During which era did dinosaurs dominate the world? (8)

10. Who is the giant with 100 eyes according to the Greek mythology? (5)

CrossWord & Search

#33

```
I N O S U M O W R E S T L I N G O C F X
T H I G S Z N C F B E G W N H L A Z A U
R D A E U N M U U N F S P H K O N O N K
F Z N O T H R U N C M P O M S P A R L A
S P S L R S R I V B X F Q I R P S M N L
F A W U E R N O M E B P G W B X A X I T
D G X K S U X E T S N D A N M U N C E P
M Y O U O A Q B K C K Q N N F E U L Y N
J R Y Z Q P G B P N I Y P T X N R B J T
J M E G K K L E L S A V X K M A N J X P
N B T R K H U B P J Z R B B C S F A I G
F F A C Q W P I W V E V F S C P F L R O
C H A R L E S D I C K E N S C A U K A I
X H E R M A N M E L V I L L E V R B Y L
K J W G R N W R R U Y X C A P A F C W K
H B S D R H P B O D R I H X M C J K D M
I E L A V T D B U S K Z O N S J X F P P
V S F F N S E T R A C S E D E N E R G H
C V H D T C S C X V K D V B O R V T V H
T E E K W R K X N T C W T D U Z Y D Q W
```

1. What is the name of the winged horse in Greek mythology? (7)

2. Who wrote Oliver Twist? (14)

3. What country did Shakespeare's Hamlet live in? (7)

4. Which book Mary Shelley wrote when she was 19? (12)

5. Who said "I think therefore I am"? (13)

6. In which book did Sherlock Holmes first show up? (14)

7. Who wrote Moby Dick? (14)

8. What is the national sport in Japan? (13)

9. What is called a yoga posture? (5)

10. Who wrote The Hunchback of Notredame? (10)

38

```
A I W H U O A H K K E E X J W S P V P X
N K W J G R O B A G X S X M I V K D E O
Z U Q H G R U B N I D E K Q X S X N A H
V O V A V J N R Q I L J U O R P I Q W C
Z Z D W Y V M T G C W E E W B L N I F I
D M E R U D Y A R D K I P L I N G R R R
Q M E I L W J B J P F L P I L A T E S T
E P Q W O Z A A Z M J S S C Z A S Q E S
T N P N V I U O I I T F C Z R E Y N W O
A G C J S J S M Y U W B E K C Y N T W K
R N N O P L T R C T T L V O P I R L K Z
A L N L B P R O U F Q H O M S W W X V E
N Z G W G X A G M B U F H H B M D L N C
T N A O P H L X S N S D A Y F P N G M W
U Z F E T D I A T N R B U K F I L P W O
L Y G O G L A M W G P A D K B A O Q B X
A I I B X X O F F O M O F P N Y L K H N
V Z K J D B F X N V A L H D Y F S T T D
Q X Y C P V P W G U A Q B J Q W B H A O
R L Q J U M S A L B W A V N W E C F D O
```

answer on page 115

1. In which sport can you win the Davis Cup? (6)

2. Which popular fitness method was invented by a German? (7)

3. Who introduced football in the world? (7)

4. Who wrote Jungle Book? (14)

5. Which animal is the symbol of cunning and dexterity? (3)

6. What is the largest bird? (7)

7. Which animal can live without food 2 years? (9)

8. Which animal does never sleep? (3)

9. What is the capital of Scotland? (9)

10. What is the only continent without active volcanoes? (9)

```
G P Z H U R A Y A F I L A H K J R U B X
W H Z E N X V L K R Q J G O E Z V U F Q
A T A U R Q G E K X C S B C Z I N E S A
W S L V A Q X O W E X J Q W J K A L L Z
R O I T L I U N D G W L X Z K M V G M M
M Q Y V L R J A M E S C O O K C G G X H
U G F J I Z Z R F P P L M O V W G R L P
R Q Y S P H W D R C A Y Y Q E D Z H E E
N T J V R B V K R K Y N S E R H O O W U
D C I B E M P L R L X N U D Y P B M Y W
F F G R T T L E L T O G B Z N X X F D M
G O G A A E C I I T F B M B S B R I J D
D M M Z C T Z N O R H V U R O E Z Z P Z
R U I I Z A U R N Z R W L E N R R A O R
H L L L Z C H O I H G W O G U Q U A O Q
U N R O S S A C N N T Z C O P F D C U S
I Y N D H K I K D F O R A Q V V W N O G
P P R T M K L Q I L P I N V F U A C B W
U M R Z Z J B N A E G R M J E J A Z K U
U K E L E N W L A P H O B W T P W H M L
```

answer on page 115

1. Which animal has got 4 stomachs? (3)

2. What country is covering 50% of the South American continent? (6)

3. Which country has more post offices than any other country? (5)

4. Which animal has got 248 brawn inside head? (11)

5. Who discovered America? (8)

6. What is tallest building in the world? (11)

7. What do people need to travel to other countries? (4)

8. Who invented the Internet? (16)

9. Who is the king of all animals? (4)

10. Who discovered Australia? (9)

```
F C F H E N V V M V R J H B V J E J N M
N J K E E C P E S U M J Z Y U E R W Y S
B I Q T N Q E E O A W Q Z P B K K R M E
H O J N I B M X F S D P F N C P Y H E J
R M W F S A D L K U P J S I M K J S Z V
S C J N U L I G P Y Z G R S B L E R N P
N Q O C O O S L T Y U Y L V D B G N E F
J B H Y M A E B A D H Z R K R P O D B D
Z L N J I H T X O R F F Y O U X U E S H
H A H L L S L I J T C F L F R Y C E E
N R A X M E H B E P E S O Y W E S Y D Y
D R R Y W Q J S L M T V U N D L H K E A
O F V J K Y Y W S T D C E A I R M W C O
A H A I V S K S S R T S V T W Y M A R Z
P Y R A E P T R E B O R G Q S R W S E I
Q K D Z B S A N B E R N A R D I N O M K
U D B A Z B U K L V H E N R Y F O R D S
A G A Q W W U M H U L W X W O B P E T Y
S I P E N K V U L S H Q M I D M Y W D B
I M Y X D D I T S L F L R M O X H R O U
```

answer on page 115

1. Which country is the birthplace of the Internet? (3)

2. Who discovered the North Pole ? (11)

3. Which car brand slogan is "the best or nothing"? (12)

4. Who made the first touch screen phone? (9)

5. What is the name of the American journal of finance and economics? (6)

6. What is the longest car in the world? (9)

7. Who was the founder of the Harvard University? (11)

8. In which city was built the first Mc Donalds? (13)

9. What is the name of the Founder of Ford Motors? (9)

10. Which country is the largest producer of wool? (9)

41

CrossWord & Search

#37

```
A F M Y U H M T Q M P C S C X V C R C P
J D L Q B R H I V I J O P B F K Q S N G
H O R F V L V B N V U J R N L E N Z P H
R Y A T S E W K W K E F C S B S X C A
Y L L P T C I A A H T V R A T U G D M F
A A E W I H R S U T I X M D Z H P L M N
E R A Z Z L A W O J E U L W S B L P A S
I P Z H R U I P O U D R I D X Z J M C B
Z G V A O S Y V M E I L M K B H N Y Y U
F B P L T R M R R E L W Y E H E L K G N
Q P A S R Q K D N S T N C B L B M E K I
M R T A Z K N Q M C K Y J Q P O K F V T
I L H Z K A C I N J D R V R W I N J I E
J B Q J X G T A C A G Z H Q P C J S E D
J C N E Y H R P D P D R T R Q X H E A S
P M L M Y S N E N A Q S R N Z A Y V K T
X A H R I L X W N N N S D Z S U A L G A
I I B I J M R O L L I N G S T O N E S T
F C A F R A N C E C X V R A T O N K I E
I J A M E S C A M E R O N N Q E Z Q B S
```

answer on page 116

1. From which country does the car brand Lexus originate? (5)

2. Who is the author of "The Three Musketeers"? (14)

3. Who is the founder of the BMW concern? (8)

4. Who was the director of the film "Avatar"? (12)

5. Who is the most expensive actor of Hollywood? (9)

6. What is the most expensive film ever made? (11)

7. Who did release an album called "A Bigger Bang"? (13)

8. In which country is lettuce the second most popular fresh vegetable? (12)

9. What is the biggest fruit? (10)

10. In what country is it possible to eat 246 varieties of cheese? (6)

```
R B G P P S N W M R G C T H S M J J P I
W N Y K L Y W C S C G O I N X Y U M I E
U V I F N U O D J X N S O G N G N P P P
O K Q X L M N C C S I M Y J E O H Z Q Z
M F W X W N O A E R V X W R P L I G R I
X V W M I K O K A U X D O C M O K G Z L
T N H A S C P P E J L Z W B J M M E R W
B M K D J F S S K E M A Y F M S R R M X
K V H R D U R W O W E E N C I I R M J G
V S Q E S Y E A G B E R Z B G E H A M K
S Z D T Q H H T Z T S Y F X A S X N Q T
O L L T S F T L H L Z T Y R X T F Y O N
L X W O L D I S P G M H I W J V O Q C U
W E F R M N W V L O X R W Q T M T R A X
J K G Z T A E N H V X A R H U N I N T Z
A Q O L J B S F E Y A E C C A N T Q S O
D T D G A K E C K X W A D V F P A T H P
Z Y P K S C E Y V E Y N Z O I P N K O Z
D O T D U O R R S U X J J J S B I Z D F
P H S Q D R Y P R L Q R N Y X M C J P Z
```

answer on page 116

1. Where was opened the first restaurant? (5)

2. What is study of earthquakes? (10)

3. Who were the Beatles? (8)

4. Who sleeps 66 % of all life ? (4)

5. What country gave us the tradition of decorating the christmas tree? (7)

6. What is the most famous movie starring Leonardo DiCaprio? (7)

7. Who is the most expensive movie actress? (16)

8. What name of the most cold city? (9)

9. Which city is the largest port in the world? (9)

10. What is the warmest sea in the world? (10)

CrossWord & Search

#39

```
F G W P J F N J B Q Q V A H T H E L H N
S A G Q R Z G Y C A B E H A H P H B U X
T I G I T H Y I D B U V Y K K O R M R D
L H M L R L P J Q E X R U M Z Y F J B E
E P W P E X P Z B R R U O I P E A B E J
V L X L S V R M F F A X O V D G L I U P
E E C M Y O E H D Q W C U C S R E Z X G
S D B A Z E N T F N U S Q L H U Y Z X W
O A S I A Y I S O S C A H A A I O J P K
O L D E O F I G J B G R M L R T N N U Y
R I M I C K E Y R O U R K E N N B A J L
N H E L E P O M Z N X Z F N Z S T F A R
I P U D M R X L E Q A N U J K E G K A H
L J N H Y W J D C L E L R V W M I C M X
K I Z N M K C O M F B J L R T A H A E L
N X B Q L Q D U P L O O C E B N D O R U
A I W J P T Y C Y W E I U O G U K F I W
R G K J A G D H D P E R K R K A J Y C C
F C Y V E J G A S T C B B X N X M A A D
B E M P V G I Z C H Q U Z T R E S M A R
```

answer on page 116

1. What is the deepest lake in the world? (6)

2. Who was the President during the attack on Pearl Harbor? (17)

3. In which country do people like to put salt in tea? (5)

4. What is the longest animated series in American TV history? (8)

5. What is the safest city in the world? (9)

6. Which football player has wun the most World Cups? (4)

7. What name of a famous actor who is also a professional boxer? (12)

8. Who was the first man to sail around the world? (8)

9. Which country won the Revolutionary War? (7)

10. Which US city is known as the City of Brotherly Love? (12)

44

```
Q V L W K A N X N E S I C F X Q P U E R
C W K F O O T B A L L N A E G U P Y E Z
Z X K Y R I N L G K Q Q E H S I N A P S
M N E T F K I F A S Q V I G U E A P M X
O Y S I V G K G S X M C U P O P Z Y A J
Z E U S Z Z X L J D Q G K X M R E Q Q S
I Z G N E F B K W M U B S F O E D H M D
L B I E L W G I C Q S S Z S W D D Y J J
L D H D E R R R R T T M E O D I R R H U
A G I F P J E L K M S D K S B S J W B X
F K T S H S V C U Q I A R T J O R A A V
I N H B A X X W S I N N K B A N H P U R
R I I Y N A J F D I Z C G X W Y M N S S
E Y B P T Y C G U Q Q F O H K E G F V R
F I G Z Y K J N R V P F M R A S K T N Q
O D U W K J W L E Y L B B P O M E U U A
X W O A W A Q O E W D T F K R E F Q E X
X W Q Z D U B R Y H T D Q L O E Y D Q B
C I Y Q J Y Q X I Z V O Z R Z J P W O T
K Y A L X O V A J E M M N W E Q J W V Z
```

answer on page 116

1. Which sport has a penalty shot? (8)

2. Which Internet browser includes "Search Engine Manager"? (14)

3. What is the mass per unit volume of material called? (7)

4. A Hybrid Tea is a type of what plant? (4)

5. Which scientist explained the concepts of gravity and motion? (11)

6. Who invented electric bulb? (6)

7. What is the first element in the periodic table? (8)

8. To which language is Portuguese closely related? (7)

9. What is the largest land animal? (8)

10. Digbeth and Edgbaston are suburbs of which British city? (10)

```
K B Q P B Q F M T P P S L B S H F P G B
S T K A W C Y K V W P T Q P G V G V J M
U L U B N A T S I X J H Y X F W Q H V F
E P N L Y I F G G D U L R R I O U U D Y
Z V H F C G K N P K H A D M N L T I H F
J R S Y L F E E Q U E R T W P H M Q U X
G M L S I L K Y E G A H M D K B K M X T
I W N D G K B R R P I A U E N D P O Q N
X Y M D L I I X E H O L R O C X J N N O
X G J A T Y S S A O L B A D W D Z G X D
D D Z K M I Z N E O E I N A F F R F N F
O X U E Q O I H C I V O F M E M M O Y S
O E D I T H P O Q A R N C D T S C I G N
N B P A C S S O D R L R G F Q B D N V O
B B S O V V R X O P R O E N L J U A N W
R Y F Y L P Z H P V U N R B E L H A E J
I X H I J E S X T M O A W I P C R M Q D
T U S B H Z T Z V P I W Q I E S K B D Z
C H J D X A V N D A I R R T N S A H B D
O X Q S O L M R A F H B Q K S D P R L U
```

answer on page 116

1. Which fruit has the highest fiber content? (11)

2. Which organ is responsible for regulating metabolism? (5)

3. Food energy is expressed in what form? (8)

4. What city lies on the western shore of the Caspian Sea? (8)

5. What sea does the Jordan River empty into? (7)

6. Where was the first newspaper published? (5)

7. What type of animal is an Oryx? (8)

8. In mythology who was the principal god of the greeks? (4)

9. On what part of the body can a tie be worn? (4)

10. What was the Roman name for England? (6)

46

```
L W Y U S P S N I O M R H X R M G O N R
L V R I P U N U A Y T L A T I Q L E B Y
T D X I V R P A B T O E T C U Y E I O C
A O D V Y P W K D H Y M U X O B R C H Y
W T H T I D N G E O U O Y Q W Z E E M M
A T P E U N F Z I N M N G N X H L E I H
P H M E R Y L L S T R E E P Q S P A C A
H G S I V J W U D P W Q N U E A Y A H R
S L C G N X B V D M Q K Y A U C O L E L
F E X D B O P B Y Z M D Z H V V B X L E
R G N K C W O C P J W Q F I B W C T A Y
L E H S I H R V D C J G Q F L S A K N D
E R K L L E Y E N R I C O F E R M I G A
X M N N N W O T E P A C Y Q Q F O P E V
Q A S U S Y V W D S Z X D Y M W E L L I
P N W J S O Y B M G J H I A E L H N O D
N Y N R X P G U F X W Q H Y P A C L U S
F Y V X F F E Z Q H C U C V Q U C G H O
K W Y M C H A R L O T T E B R O N T E N
G G J X L T C F J U T O R U H O J O I P
```

answer on page 116

1. Meyer, Eureka and Sorrento are types of which yellow citrus fruit? (5)

2. Which actress played Margaret Thatcher in The Iron Lady? (12)

3. Salt Lake City is the captial city of which US state? (4)

4. In which country did the poodle breed of dog originate? (7)

5. Which renaissance sculptor created the statue of David? (12)

6. The UEFA Champions League Final was won by which British club? (7)

7. Who made the first nuclear reactor? (11)

8. Which US motorbike company is known by the initials "HD"? (14)

9. Which South African city is known as "Mother City"? (8)

10. Which English author wrote the novel "Jane Eyre"? (15)

```
I H U N K Z V K Y O F O K R B R E T A Y
A P B L O O P R E V I L K K O G A Y I D
L B N D E S T J T C W I F L M L O X D U
C R A L X Y L Z N J B D E U D Y L Y R S
C R E H O Y Y D U T Y L Y H E R L O J U
G Y B T B C A R T U E B J Z B T I N P E
Y O E T W Q G M V Z M N K J M B L K Q A
D R E Y R D R T Y Z O E G V K P F G X M
A K F A Y A A P S E A C B L R U G S F Y
H S F R E Z P L B B X B F L A A V M K W
L H O A N Y N Z M J N D I G W N U P E T
C I C Q S I I Q P I G H U G Z E D V F E
R R N H I P D I N R R Y R L W S G L W Y
T E Y M D F A K A I N R O F I L A C C K
W H S B T W R N F N S T J F H R D Z T Q
F V D W L M W Q I V Y Q D T Q Y U S J I
B H X M A V P N E S P F S Q Q B E I U J
F S M J W O N L J C H G U D K I P X D T
R Q J K D R I S M U R L Y R Y L Z M G R
I D E T I N U R E T S E H C N A M G S N
```

answer on page 117

1. Which English football club has the most followers? (16)

2. The Royal Albert Dock is found in which UK city? (9)

3. John Bull is a national personification of which country? (7)

4. By area, which is the largest county in England? (9)

5. Which Marvel superhero has the real name Dr. Robert Bruce Banner? (4)

6. Arabica, Robusta and Liberica are types of which bean? (10)

7. Sacramento is the capital of which US state? (10)

8. Which language has the more native speakers? (7)

9. Who was the Ancient Greek God of the Sun? (6)

10. Who has won the most total Academy Awards? (10)

```
S R P D B O G E W O U D F U H N G T J S
Q G A Z P B L S V H H K U L W M S U E V
I W H R M O A X E P A Q N B T M M W Q R
X T X D G X F G I Y M V S P Y E K N Z Y
X Z D Z R S R J Y X E U X E X Z Z H H Q
N E I V N A Q Q H G K Z L I P H I B S E
V G U N S E D D V L F L C F W X U D O J
E I X R B O D G B Z O O S C H I Z M G M
N H B N B X B E D W S U Z W T H G N S I
U X U L J P Q P W L O I G X K O H B L C
S R J O L N D M K S U U F W P C A Y T R
B Z F K N Q A N E R T L Y P W X P B D O
P C A L L I G R A P H Y B Y T E V L A S
Q I L C Q I I U B T A A K M O A Z H M O
Y T T N Z K F T W A F R K H Q Q Z H P F
L F I X Y Z H F L W R I A I N A Z N A T
O K V H O J F P C A I T X M O E I A K V
E L Z J C A I J D Z C A X T K M M A W V
O H E J N Z H D B M A O N V X F C D S V
U Z B Z H Z Q Z L C K I Y T H F D R B F
```

answer on page 117

1. Aureolin is a shade of what colour? (6)

2. Which planet in the Milky Way is the hottest? (5)

3. What company was initially know as "Blue Ribbon Sports"? (4)

4. What art form is described as "decorative handwriting"? (11)

5. In what country would you find Mount Kilimanjaro? (8)

6. What software company is headquartered in Redmond, Washington? (9)

7. What is the largest Spanish speaking city in the world? (6)

8. Which is the only body part that is fully-grown from birth? (4)

9. In what country was Elon Musk born? (11)

10. What country has the most islands? (6)

```
V K F L G G P N X B Q D T F K R S Q T H
J P W C Y T J Y U G H A T G V V L Y Q E
J T Y P B N O V A H W C Z M R P A Y M L
Q F U M N P A O B A X V M D I J P L Q W
O Y Q G A S W B Z I C G S E Q J E X X T
S W E E V N P D L J C G P M S J N X I I
D J A F W D W J Z A K L L Z G P V C D A
C S R J J O O N C U T Y X Q J N R U U K
G P K P T W T T N T M B L U Q Y O D B Y
G T F T A C A B A Z J L L J G F H Y L L
X I A W W H S V H C O T B N B G H X I H
E W A T K J R G E V I S F C P J L B N Z
A V D E S C Z I S Y E T E W D O Q P K N
L O C O P E N H A G E N C U D Z M Y I K
B O D A R O L O C X C F O R J J K E H D
P Q M G Q M M Z E F X Q H L A D U N C W
Z T H Z U L C O P R X N Z N M T U T H J
V R H O D E I S L A N D O D B K N N V E
A L E U Z E N E V N H B I G N U Q A Q K
S H S G K V U U U D Q S F J F G Q S C B
```

answer on page 117

1. Where is the strongest human muscle located? (3)

2. Which river flows through the Grand Canyon? (8)

3. Where is the largest waterfall in the world located? (9)

4. What is the state capital of New York? (6)

5. On what continent would you find the world's largest desert? (10)

6. What is the capital of Ireland? (6)

7. What is the smallest US state by area? (11)

8. What is the capital of Canada? (6)

9. In what capital would you find The Little Mermaid statue? (10)

10. What is the only flag that does not have four sides? (5)

```
P Y X E V P Q P P V O V V A N R G M T I
E X S S E N N I U G B L J J W O Q B P Q
E M C L R A A I T R Q K K G R U H X R Z
O D C Q R X N Z R Z J W G B X Y C S L X
M G B F P A I X T G Y W I S N U H F V B
D Y E E Y D H Z X P I L S M R X J V O E
F E S I P N C X O C U Q D X B C D K Y A
N Q Z S D S X J H F F N J I V L Z N N C
R O G B X D G Y P J B K D P J T E G U M
Y S Y O Q N G Y M N A S T I C S S D N L
L V Z X S B L K D N V J L G I T L X O D
L Y I Y L C Y G O P W X Q T R I A E L N
M N S K M R I T W R Y B W O X S V T H O
P P F T B E L T W E Z Z M I W P R M R W
B W I L G A B Q A C Q F G M Z Z A W B J
F F N V D J O T A M J D J J X U J O Z G
R B L P Q N B L Q P O O Z A E E D Q I W
P C A G J O Q B Z B P R Z B I S E X S E
P I N J W M O S R Z X L H H N V P P B A
J O D O W D F I X J P Y E C W Z Z Q Y W
```

answer on page 117

1. Where did sushi originate? (5)

2. What is the world's best selling stout beer? (8)

3. What country drinks the most coffee? (7)

4. Pink Ladies and Granny Smiths are types of what fruit? (5)

5. Simone Biles is famous for her skill in what sport? (10)

6. What was the first name of Argentinian soccer star Maradona? (5)

7. What sporting event has a strict dress code of all white? (9)

8. What is the science of colors? (10)

9. Who founded the branch of science known as spectroscopy? (8)

10. Who is the father of the concept of atom? (6)

```
E P B H C M N P G H Y R J A H Y Q X T M
P V M A W Z E S W V F W U K Y Z P R U J
G H G C D H P X A F B O U K B J J B G K
A C S C N H Q T C N K T W Z N R Z Q B N
D L O Z M E D I T E R R A N E A N K B S
C Z B W D P T O B B E J H A C V V E A A
R F N V O I I U E L T D W D B R G N L A
O I V W B C B A C T E R I A U N G A M C
V U P U L P B X Q V O K E W U A N L N C
W I L L I A M W O R D S W O R T H N R F
U V V P N J K C N Z I N Q H V T T E E P
D F Z W T C K J P G N X H F I A A L W T
B P E Y S A R L Q I U P A C E H H L O B
H Z R N E P O H Q G V K M M T N O A T Y
D I H L E I Y L G G H Z A C N A A R L B
R Y V N O T W E N C A A S I A M T I E K
Y U P Q M O E O O U G F A D M Y C S F A
Q O A Z Z L N J L M B X A Y F U E F F V
O N P K S U M E H G T R H L D U H N I B
R X Y R C S J C E J D X S I S Y O T E M
```

answer on page 117

1. Who was the first to study the solar system? (11)

2. Where does the US Congress meet? (7)

3. Who was the stamp distributor who became a great poet? (17)

4. Which country was known previously as Indo China? (7)

5. In which sea does Malta lie? (13)

6. Where is the Statue of Liberty situated? (7)

7. Which is the world's most visited site? (11)

8. Who was the promoter of paperback? (12)

9. What did the Dutch scientist Leeuwenhoek invent? (8)

10. What island is New York on? (9)

52

```
C V H O I I A Y H Q K G L U M K J E X W
Y N S F T L H E D S S E S S Y B G U W B
O A I Z A T U L A B E L T A S M A N G Y
F D F R L N E D Z J A F K P O B P K T H
Q Q Y B A D S R I I Q X J R G U L A A C
R N R G R J A Z P R X U J Z K Z I T G Z
X W C L J E H U G J N Z S P L R Q R H N
R S X V P X S X R P L B F C E T T R M X
I F A H L R B A Z Z Y P N B W U R Q A A
N F F M A H L R D P E A I Q U K E M X M
Y S C M Q W Y F B H C L T D M A S G E M
G N P J D Y M I H I Q Q Z E E H E Q P S
Y U C Z L Q W M T F G L F Q V Y D B T W
E R R H A S W A J R W L M P A X A S A D
P G L C N A V S D S S F O H M M L I A
P Y M I M R O C S I C N A R F N A S G S
E Y B P B M X F R X H S H C U B C J G J
L S Z L A H V C Q J I T X W W V A O S B
L D F I I E V W W M G H O Y L K T Q D K
A U H W R L K C T B U Q M F C W A G T F
```

answer on page 117

1. Where can you find "Golden Gate" bridge? (12)

2. Which animal is called the 'old man of the sea'? (5)

3. What is the type of Animals with pouches to carry their young ones? (10)

4. Through which organ do humans produce sound? (6)

5. Where is the driest place in the world? (13)

6. Which is the largest palace in the world? (7)

7. Which country has the same flag as of USA? (7)

8. Blue revolution refers to the production of what? (4)

9. Who discovered New Zeland? (10)

10. Which place is known as Venice of East? (8)

53

```
O H B Z N B A C U V H N E X F H A K P R
R W E O I H G O M T W U S D J P H R I E
A O T R H A A M M N V Q E G W V T A C J
J U C I L D T T G K V B N Q O V E M W F
N Z Y V E Q H G K F W S I Z Z T B N L R
A Q O J D H A F X R H D H U S T A E U B
M L C N W N C E B H T N C Y P T Z D E D
I K F M E V H F R R V W S M C N I U V U
L E I H N O R I V L Q E I Q S F L O Z R
I N L O C N I L M A H A R B A Z E L L H
K Z T E Q Y S S U C S A M A D D N I E E
T U G H P O T U Z S H B N D Y C E A X V
N Y J T Y M I N N O O F W O A X E Y J G
U W U V M C E N U P A K R R C N U T F F
O V O W C E S U J Y G T O B F K Q C E I
M T T P Z P P Y J F Y T P S Z S Z T I S
Y T M I Q M Q A K K E C V O Y L L Y E S
A Q C B O J U U D N Q P J Y B R S U V D
L X J Y B F J S E X L Y A L K J B F E U
W R L B A N K E R G R J E O C J C U C V
```

answer on page 118

1. Who abolished slavery in America? (14)

2. Where was the first Asian Games held? (8)

3. The oldest inhabited capital city in the world? (8)

4. What pigment is in carrots? (8)

5. Which football player is known as "Black Pearl"? (4)

6. In whose books is Miss. Marple, the amateur detective? (14)

7. Who were the first to notice that a snowflake has six sides? (7)

8. Which is the first country to have adopted a national flag? (7)

9. What is the name of Britain's most luxurious ocean liner? (14)

10. Which is the largest volcano in the world? (16)

54

```
Y N N D P J N X N S B L N P K I A L F B
I Z D Z C M H O P P K B N H V W O Q G F
F O J D G U R I I V F O S G B N L B W B
I D S E N T P Y E S A X E T I S L Y Q R
W F Q X C A X L N K P J B T U J T S B F
A M Z E T U L V A K C F E P E G F S K F
J Y L I D W T K B N E R C U A G A P Z W
T E Q K L F I M C E T H Q R I Y L N F Q
P A K Y H S I G Q U V A M X N X Y T D G
N A G I H C I M Q N A E I I F J B B I A
E Y G O L O Y H T H C I R N S K Y D J J
A O O R C H I D S Z Y D D L S P F W H J
L S P W T J O J U E C X L S Y E Q Y Z Q
M O Q G K D M G Y F D V P E A H C V Q H
X I S Z P N D N C D E Z F X W T I L U J
Y L G U O N N E P C Z Q N A Y W M L Z O
Q R N L F Q W O I R K G P W P N O P L P
V T I W F D D X J K B Y U M P L X N S S
Y U T F Q F Z D F R F C F A B G L Z Z Z
W V W S I X B B T P M A O O O W Z K X I
```

answer on page 118

1. Which vegetable is a green variety of banana? (8)

2. What type of flowers produce vanilla pods? (7)

3. What is the other name of vitamin A? (7)

4. Which one of the five Great Lakes lies totally within the United States? (8)

5. What is the science of the natural history of fish called? (11)

6. What is the name of the negatively charged particle in an atom? (8)

7. What Los Angeles community is noted for celebrities and mansions? (12)

8. Which country has the largest capacity reservoir in the world? (6)

9. What U.S. state has the most counties? (5)

10. Which is New Zealand's largest city? (8)

```
B Q C K A J Z L N P F R V A A C O U L H
R H D A X F Z E I M B I K A E T C B T W
W S Q J O A Z Y J U Z M R H B Z K R R I
X E D E U R F K I S A A C N E W T O N L
B Q G M R Z M E B E E L H Z Q A B U C K
M X Z S K M L H M K Y C M S B X M V X V
H H W W V W P S H U X G K U X D T N W S
W V G J U O X L G S R F R Q O B S G J J
C C Q E H G X P I F U E F E B W G O T N
S B B S P W U N Y N J P A D N M K K V W
Z A J L K O B U A A P C F Y L E S D A U
X M S W Z H E N U U X U G Q S U A E K S
C G L I G H T P E N S P P K I P C U Y F
P Y O E R E U E B R I T G E H H N I K S
Q M K G T N A B A S I A R F U F Q C A Q
M O A N Z R U R N E H W M I F P E O M F
A Q U K X B P X W A K U X B A D X S N F
R O U S C J K R U E I H S A P T Y R E J
M M R W I H R E C W W F T G J D S X I M
N R O T I N O M N Q Z X H M N C W T X T
```

answer on page 118

1. Who proved the existence of seven colors in sunlight? (11)

2. What is the name of the highest active volcano in Europe? (9)

3. In which country Adolf Hitler was born? (7)

4. Which input device has a connection with the touch screen? (8)

5. What do mitochondria produce? (6)

6. What is the most sensitive organ in the human body? (4)

7. The longest bone of the human body is what? (5)

8. Where is the human body's weakest muscle located? (3)

9. The longest coastline is seen in which continent? (4)

10. The users can see information on which part of the computer? (7)

```
S G R W V R E W J D S U C O W J M E Z W
T R F H C K B D Y X Q Q N F R K J R I F
N Y R K H A Q W B Y C V K U W Q X U I Y
O O O U K M W F M B I Q J L E H U N E S
Z P T A S E A O F B Y M Z L X I L G D K
O C B D I K L Q B O A E F K I Y B B Y W
Y R D S D G Y A I V Z T M A I B T C C N
Z Z P O Y I R U U X K S P D O L P H I N
J B T K P M M S R A G Y A O J I E E P S
S J Z U P T J T O S V S H K V Z T Y E S
R P Q Q O R C R N L R G N E P A L Q Q C
I F I I L W S A F D O N F R E C T N I V
R B F W A K L X I T I O U O K E R L G
R B S M O V V I V O A T V U I F C I C T
K C F U Z I J A E R U A B S U D W H I K
E I L G W J B Q Y E Q R P I Y O T Z N Y
S I M Q J E A C E T E E Y A Q L M Q F Q
J W A J X U O P U S T P D X L W S E F X
O N L T Q C W H A A O O C Q I K Q W B B
E M N O C L A F E N I R G E R E P V G L
```

answer on page 118

1. Where we find Tropical Rainforests? (7)

2. Which one is the secondary memory device? (10)

3. What is a rocky object orbiting the sun? (8)

4. Which bird is the fastest in the world? (15)

5. Which country faces the most number of earthquakes on the earth? (5)

6. Who is "The father of the Internet?" (8)

7. Which instructs the computer to use its components? (15)

8. Mount Everest is located in which country? (5)

9. New Holland is known as what? (9)

10. Which creature sleeps with open one eye? (7)

```
B Y H K R O M X B S Z A G G A P T Q A D
Y L C L O U Y X T C H Y Z G J C Q T A B
P Z K K F G P K U D Y U Z W L I F X H J
Y E P B K A G E M L B C N G F I Z N L P
I G I C Y Y G F T R N F F G M T V E P W
D I B C E Q R N Y Y R S S L A G V J Y X
A C I R E M A H T R O N M A M R E I G I
Q Z C I F E H G S B U E J R F L Y X G D
P C W E V K R A M N E D T P I R M T G Z
B B U K I G C K R L U M U H E X I N L M
N I Q G T P R W M K Y P C N Q I Y C E W
K P P H G Z V K A W V J D Z L D Q M A G
I N O R T H S E A J D U T N R D F O N L
I F U H C C I P U H C A M Y A K L L F C
R V K Z V I I C H K F D S I N L N N K J
G M I C H A E L F A R A D A Y S E O E B
S W Y G G G B P Z N O C E K G P U R Y E
N X B F Z P T A M S V G R E E C E I I O
U Z H G M K T D B H L T M I J X C K R V
Y M L U I R V W H A E A M N K B M B W J
```

answer on page 118

1. What is the other name of Eire? (7)

2. What sea separates Scandinavia from Britain? (8)

3. The Straits of Magellan divide which country? (5)

4. On which peak of Peru is the magnificent city of the Incas located? (11)

5. Who propounded the theory of electrolysis? (14)

6. Atlas Mountain is found in which continent? (6)

7. Where is the Sonoran desert located? (12)

8. The Faeroe Islands is found in which country? (7)

9. Mount Olympus is found where? (6)

10. Budapest is the capital of which country? (7)

CrossWord & Search

#54

```
Z R S G I B U T T W S N B J N Y W V O H
M C Y T K V M G T A D G F U P G K J U O
O I S J R S L A I R E A Q T C C I A L B
A U K X U A K U N L S S A I B M A Z V F
F Z J M N B T N F D R O N N G Y P G H X
W F H R P D M O W W V Y Z A A E I M R M
J P W X E A U K S O L S N N M T E G D E
K E X H F S X C H P Y Y K O G S U A N R
Q I A R U L S U Q V H T Q W Z S A H J C
I E O M V Z G E S B W E A R D N U T B U
R D A R Q S M F U N R B R E Z L D E E R
W G J F R S B F H D O S H E I F G B L Y
D L S P J U C M G C K V U F Y Q I R Z S
Y V O U T I B G M A E R T S F L U G G P
U I Q R J D Q S N G R Y Y G R Z M T R F
D R F X C A A Z B Z M Y R N D C T R Z C
K E X B Q C R P P L L J Y P B J V E Q Q
F C K I D D A M C O S M O L O G Y S V X
K G R E A T B E A R L A K E Q R J G I J
H L P S N E H T A S W N A G U U E E P P
```

answer on page 118

1. What is the name of the largest lake in Canada? (13)

2. Copper Belt is found in which country? (6)

3. Which planet is the smallest in the whole solar system? (7)

4. What is the oldest capital city in the world? (6)

5. What is the name of the warm sea current from the Gulf of Mexico? (10)

6. What sea separates New Zealand and Australia? (9)

7. What is known as the study of the Universe? (9)

8. What is "Cold Deserts"? (6)

9. The upper layer of the atmosphere is known as what? (12)

10. The Dragon Kingdom is another name of which country? (6)

59

CrossWord & Search

#55

G	U	V	W	C	P	R	N	I	Q	G	G	U	L	W	G	G	L	C	B
L	J	T	L	L	P	Z	E	S	W	T	X	B	B	S	P	T	A	Y	U
V	V	F	A	Y	B	T	D	L	I	X	Z	O	M	U	R	N	C	L	T
Z	G	N	L	M	X	D	I	Z	Z	O	T	M	L	W	A	W	I	S	T
B	T	P	L	E	I	D	L	B	B	S	R	U	V	E	Y	R	R	U	E
S	H	U	S	L	B	R	G	K	W	L	A	V	L	B	I	E	E	C	R
E	F	Y	D	O	K	C	F	A	Z	V	H	M	X	W	N	P	H	P	F
L	H	R	C	T	K	O	N	X	X	X	R	P	Q	C	G	T	P	C	L
Y	C	G	N	P	F	A	P	O	U	Z	J	E	P	Q	M	I	S	M	I
Z	M	O	N	G	O	L	O	I	D	C	R	J	G	O	A	L	F	Z	E
W	E	T	F	A	I	I	V	C	A	N	D	R	Y	J	N	I	P	W	S
A	G	H	O	A	G	S	M	J	D	W	O	S	E	G	T	A	P	P	G
A	R	A	B	Y	P	A	C	W	G	J	P	C	V	D	I	H	F	V	L
S	C	A	S	P	I	A	N	S	E	A	T	Q	Z	X	S	B	Z	N	A
X	K	O	L	N	L	E	K	E	G	F	M	K	J	C	J	S	K	H	L
B	R	H	P	I	U	X	X	D	Y	C	D	C	A	B	I	R	I	P	G
L	P	M	O	U	F	U	K	B	R	W	W	C	S	B	T	E	M	Z	A
M	Y	Q	M	M	E	U	G	N	D	Y	I	M	S	X	R	L	L	J	K
Q	B	V	Y	U	U	P	D	U	E	K	J	K	L	S	W	L	N	D	D
D	F	M	O	L	T	X	C	C	S	N	U	D	V	O	Q	K	H	A	D

1. The best caviar in the world is associated with which water body? (10)

2. The Kalahari Desert is found in which country? (8)

3. What is the shape of the Earth? (9)

4. What was the name of the ancient Greek astronomer? (7)

5. What were the first living things appear on the earth? (6)

6. Which race forms the largest group of people? (9)

7. What is the only insect that can turn its head? (13)

8. What is studied by a lepidopterist? (11)

9. The largest rodent in the world is what? (8)

10. The tortoise belongs to which class of animals? (8)

60

```
D B J F P G I A N T S Q U I D A Y Z Z O
Q F B R I S O D V X O I R A B D Y C A B
P E A G E Z N E I M W Q V K Z R I E R E
W T C Q C D M I D O Q M B I E B S S W T
I H Q B I J N M F L C U Y Y B M K O W Y
D Z F X U S V A Q D E T O X E E L O D J
A M B E P W P A M R O R D A A E A M N E
Q C Z K Z O C F Q A A Z W I I L I V R D
Z L E N D K H Z T C L K C F Y K L O E S
M V D A C A K M S E W A D Z P G V Z N R
A V X N R C K A R N Z J S G B I C E B Q
N C B E P X G S L Y P T E T N D Z L T Z
D H K J K A L I Q M K J D M N Y L E Q K
R I V Z D I B Z T D C E O T H A X N B A
I Q M A S A A T F X M I A B D E I Q J R
L Q M S C K F G I C X L L C J X L G J A
L X O I M H R G K S J G Z B J W A N L D
X F M G G D I N O S A U R U Z V O C S E
R Y Y G M J C S B R S Q U S S T I G V S
G M D O S J A V B G W S Q O G V B D G C
```

answer on page 119

1. Which is the largest monkey in the world? (8)

2. What is the name of the deer family's largest member? (5)

3. What type of animal eats both animals and plants? (8)

4. What is the largest amphibian in the world? (15)

5. Which animal has the largest eyes in the world? (10)

6. What is Canada's national animal? (6)

7. Which is the best known prehistoric animal? (8)

8. Which are the remains of prehistoric life? (7)

9. Sahara desert is located in which Continent? (6)

10. Where is the largest chameleon found? (10)

```
M U Y Z L F S U P J G F U I M Y P T L I
Y Z L G P D L M C M W V O V B K Y R D N
S L A G M V F G D U Z Z S X B Z A V Q Y
D E J G A L B E R T E I N S T E I N B W
U O L G M G Y R V P V E D Y Y W A I R
A N U R F G J B X Z M V B H H E J K N T
S A Y J Y S O V K S Q Y P R A L Q O D J
S R F E P N P Q I Q L A L H N J V X N C
U D J L S K S N M O R C Z M U R B K W Y
T O M A L N A G X G J J N P J S S O T Q
E D I N Q M M K O J O J A I C H U Y D A
M A F K U E J H X V I J G T X P S T S W
A V X H W O T D R M U D R H I I Q F E A
D I R X Q I R B L H U N I C R G G J V C
A N K H L F F I K D F N A A Z J H E R F
M C R B Y K R U G Q V S P B B G R C O I
G I P E Q J O H X A S W N M C G A F V F
Z N F Z M B S G C O M L U Q J F R G E Y
L N M N D O M T K N D I C B D M Z S L M
X E N G A K R J C I G F Q T V J Y Q Q U
```

answer on page 119

1. What is the Japanese art of cultivating dwarf trees called? (6)

2. Which famous Spanish painter is known as the father of modern art? (7)

3. What is the name of London's famous wax museum? (14)

4. Who first measured the velocity of light? (5)

5. What is the name of the art of folding paper into decorative forms? (7)

6. Which famous Italian artist and inventor designed the helicopter? (15)

7. The Theory of Relativity was proposed by whom? (14)

8. In which European city the Eiffel Tower located? (5)

9. Which school of thought coincided with the Renaissance? (8)

10. What is the art of drawing or paintings on stone called? (11)

CrossWord & Search

#58

answer on page 119

T	H	F	G	Z	U	H	D	H	R	G	W	A	F	M	H	F	Y	T	W
K	H	J	W	C	P	R	O	I	V	V	S	J	N	V	T	F	V	K	P
K	L	G	L	U	L	D	I	J	P	B	B	T	C	I	R	G	Y	E	J
J	M	O	I	R	M	A	V	Z	X	L	N	N	H	E	M	O	E	B	U
C	J	V	S	R	L	Q	B	X	I	O	V	V	N	I	A	C	P	S	
P	C	I	I	A	W	W	T	P	L	S	I	Y	C	H	B	N	L	K	L
I	Z	B	E	N	N	D	Z	C	S	O	S	S	U	N	L	H	W	S	A
R	N	V	D	Z	C	G	Y	T	V	L	C	S	H	K	F	P	D	B	I
F	H	E	Y	F	H	E	E	O	I	N	F	Z	S	I	N	O	J	G	H
F	W	Z	G	F	D	G	N	L	L	V	O	T	N	H	O	O	D	M	X
W	K	B	D	V	T	V	L	T	E	L	S	A	T	U	R	N	D	F	A
K	R	L	E	A	D	B	B	G	V	S	K	E	W	G	C	O	B	L	D
Y	N	E	G	A	H	P	G	B	X	A	B	N	A	Z	T	I	L	B	D
T	A	N	G	O	K	H	B	Y	L	F	N	M	A	O	V	B	N	B	G
B	N	Q	L	S	T	K	W	U	I	P	H	G	N	R	T	G	I	C	E
U	W	D	J	T	M	T	X	U	H	L	I	J	O	M	F	V	W	X	W
N	K	W	E	E	B	M	Y	K	T	R	Z	V	C	G	U	M	B	M	U
N	Y	D	G	M	Z	N	V	P	T	L	W	I	N	N	H	F	H	W	Y
Y	J	E	K	O	J	Q	I	V	P	O	T	G	L	V	F	Q	I	V	O
U	H	K	C	C	T	M	H	F	A	N	L	C	F	G	O	T	W	T	C

1. What is the most notable feature of a pelican? (4)

[ ][ ][ ][ ]

2. Which is the main source of energy to earth? (3)

[ ][ ][ ]

3. Who was the architect of The Guggenheim Museum in New York? (16)

[ ][ ][ ][ ][ ][ ][ ][ ][ ][ ][ ][ ][ ][ ][ ][ ]

4. Who made the painting The Starry Night? (14)

[ ][ ][ ][ ][ ][ ][ ][ ][ ][ ][ ][ ][ ][ ]

5. Where was Leonardo DiCaprio born? (10)

[ ][ ][ ][ ][ ][ ][ ][ ][ ][ ]

6. Which animal is the subject of Goodnight Moon? (5)

[ ][ ][ ][ ][ ]

7. What was the subject of the earliest known paintings? (7)

[ ][ ][ ][ ][ ][ ][ ]

8. What is the name for a traditional Argentine music and dance? (5)

[ ][ ][ ][ ][ ]

9. Which planet has the largest number of satellite? (6)

[ ][ ][ ][ ][ ][ ]

10. Which Celestial body has the most concentric orbit? (5)

[ ][ ][ ][ ][ ]

63

```
J J M R O W M J B S Y E Q J J O Y N B C
O P B J Y H E W U N G Q I A Z X G E G N
J O Z F D U R T Y B Q M L H O E U N A C
W R Y W N S T A S N O N L Y G O K M F R
E I S M A R H M L D A T M U I N A T I T
I U Z D X R D W G J R M J C D T D B P Z
L S J T K N X O G F T P R P M L F E V M
B X N O O E G R W S K E A E A S A S M O
B S Y L A J O F I C O P F X G K M Q J L
D Z H U G W X K K O E B U M Z O Q W S I
S Y P G N K T F N E N D W N K T M T P V
C A M P X Y T N L F P E P N M N H C H E
W J J E A M G B A C C E L E R A T O R R
L O D I L Z X K O H D E S E H U V I G E
D A R J O O R H E O O U W D N O O U X V
N F Y G N A T R L Q X O Z V B N Q W K A
Z H N S N A Q P U O I G B L Z H E C A N
M I B S Q Q H M B E E T L E Z U T I E S
D B W R P I E V Q E V C F L B Q F T T K
O I Y I N I Y Y A J D G O J T H S S V E
```

answer on page 119

1. Which is the element found on the surface of the moon? (8)

2. What is the unit of time based on the orbit of the Earth around the sun? (4)

3. Who is known as the founder of "Geo Centric Theory"? (7)

4. Mercedes cars belong to which country? (7)

5. Who built the first American self-propelled steam vehicle? (11)

6. Who constructed an Internal Combustion Engine? (13)

7. What part or device is used to control the speed of a vehicle? (11)

8. What is the name for the wild dog of Australia? (5)

9. Which animal has the widest hearing range? (7)

10. What class of creature has the most species? (6)

```
P W L L A Y E K M U M B T G Z U A S T O
C S X K W G V U T F D D O I L W S U V M
I H J A R F O G R N H U Y C P N X V R T
Z L F L F F D V J E B V P E M U U O C S
P Q C G F R L J K S V C Y M K L G H N H
X I B B S X I N W Z D V B L E K I L C E
F V V A X Z E C I U U Z R A V N P A N L
N U M H Q E Z E A F F J H R A R K Y L S
D I G L H H V F Z C U P E O W B K K Y I
Q Q V E F V R X I W A Y L C I X W L V L
W X U S C C N U D R F Z F K Q B V V X V
J H N I S I E Y X B J E T E U Z E U Y E
H F K G C S N P A Z Q U B F D G H J V R
H S R N P B E E T B M Q Y E O B D Q L S
D G S W H Y O L V Q D S Y L F T M N L T
B V I Q O F O Q P K S P T L J V A D K E
U F T E Y K B M B P V Y D E O U Y F R I
D T V C Q D X W K S A B R R M R M A L N
Z D X X N L K J G B M H T T X M S P V V
P A A K M O N T E C A R L O R A L L Y M
```

answer on page 119

1. What is the largest joint in the human body? (4)

2. What was the rally with which the World Rally Championship opened? (15)

3. What animal often symbolizes peace in art? (4)

4. Who wrote The Giving Tree? (15)

5. Which millionaire industrialist started in Cleveland? (11)

6. Who made the painting The School of Athens? (7)

7. Which company manufactures the iPad? (5)

8. In which European city can you ride in a gondola, a type of boat? (6)

9. Which country conducted the first civil service examination of the world? (5)

10. What is the only continent with land in all four hemispheres? (6)

```
E C A F J S X G L P U R T D Z D E R L B
M I A R B O A L D H Z M Z V X U U I F O
G L V E K P B R E H T K A A Q E G Z V T
T B O T X M A P Z V M K H N Z F F H C H
G A M I H K V R K N A U M J D J C R Z T
I S J N L N U A I U R P A L C N J U U N
O Q V A P E H F K S C F L W G D A K T A
G N I E K T X T B W E B A T C H U K T K
T G I G H G A A L I L M R V S G U I W D
T H Q B V I K U U U L L I Z U E G S J M
E P H A L K L N W A O C A J G K M Y Z I
T Z W R G A P N Z Y M U L C X J M Q V G
O X J I J P C M P O A S P J H N S L R S
V P I A H B D C K H L J V B Z B S H E K
P F C O I W Z P M C P X V V J R E Z V G
V E E C N A L A B H I V N F N C M V U X
A J Y D Y K K S A D G A W V P K H X U Y
B A R J Z Y W O Q I H E V I F L C E H C
M A D S I T Z A X O I J P J V H D J Y V
Z H Q R Q F U Z W D C Q O Y D R D A W F
```

answer on page 120

1. In which European city is the Elysee Palace situated? (5)

2. Where is the tibia found? (3)

3. What is the name of a deadly mosquito-borne disease? (7)

4. How many basic tastes can humans sense? (4)

5. What is the part of the eye where the image must be focused? (6)

6. What sensory function do the ears provide other than hearing? (7)

7. What is the word for a person with very pale skin and eyes? (6)

8. Who founded the science of microscopic anatomy? (16)

9. Who first put forward the nebular hypothesis of origin of solar system? (4)

10. Where on the human body is the mandible located? (4)

```
S M Z H D T J Z K Z P I D K T Z F F Z W
L A H O R E T S I L H P E S O J P R J U
O N M M D D B Y N A X G L S O X Y G E N
Z D B N Z A T H A W K Y P V I W X C Y C
K R W D O H G U I T Y C W Z U X A U R F
F E L W H U C Z R H W S M U E P B P B C
J A J N R X W A T R Y O P F V R Y G D O
P S J H N K E L R O Y R Q X D A U H S B
B V M S U H H N L O O X B R I Z D G R P
Y E T I Y Q A C Y T V U O O Q W T A E Y
A S G U I Q L Z E O K Q N K A H A N B X
P A I V N U Q I R E D M N O T I M R J T
D L Z M F F N G R V F H B S O E F F V S
F I H E A V A A N U C L E U S D Y I T C
H U N M J N T O R X T H R S J I N Q T
L S U Y N I C F N Z C N P O U O Q Q Z A
D A J Z N A T B N D P R N T T Y F N J B
K O T Z N X F Y X F X R Y T Q Q F Y B G
K T N S Y G O L O T S O R G A B J O G T
I H R D V E E N C I R L S P J F M Y K D
```

answer on page 120

1. What is the science of grasses called? (11)

2. Which gas is evolved during photosynthesis? (6)

3. Where is the esophagus located? (5)

4. Who introduced the antiseptic principle into surgery? (12)

5. What is the name of the tissue group? (5)

6. What is the control centre of the cell? (7)

7. What is the main organ of the cardiovascular system? (5)

8. What protein is found in skin, hair and nails? (7)

9. What does the golgi apparatus store? (7)

10. Who wrote and illustrated the first comprehensive textbook of anatomy? (15)

```
H A Q Y N N N S Z J D E H G Y H L O I G
A J I P A N A S G E O T H A X X J F Z N
M I H E Q L N C N O O M O E W H E A Q S
H R M C Q W K A I S L O M E T M P K E E
V R T L L D R Q W O B A O D J L W N K O
L V P U W B G X O D N P S T H L O S L V
C U U H M C S B W T Y D A U U I I Y D J
X H Q E I P U J H C T Z P A T L H T J A
X U M P Q F I R W F C N I C B O Y M G V
Q X A G K E O A X G O R E T L G S T D J
F L D S T P M T I Y E T N M O S Y I I J
N E V R O U Z H G T O Q S L X D B X B R
W Y N L O Y P O C R H U O N N M K W S T
S N O G G J L A P N E T C D Q M X Z H F
H G Y T I O B Z T B S O H W V R F E W C
Y Z K L I O R H A I A G I I N N V D Q K
E G N S N Q R T H M G M J J U E Y O L D
P G Y A Y K L K J S I W C R J D C S W U
K H Y A I A N W I O F J E H P V W J M D
P C D I S G Q D J C W N O Q A B K J Q H
```

answer on page 120

1. Which is the first oxygen producing Organism? (13)

2. What is the function of connective tissue? (10)

3. What is the scientific name of the human species? (11)

4. What is liquid connective tissue called? (5)

5. Which human bones connected with neck? (5)

6. What science studies the structural and cultural features of a person? (12)

7. Who is the author of the book "Man's Place in Nature"? (6)

8. What is the study of tissue called? (9)

9. What protects the cell's contents? (8)

10. What science studies the structure and functions of the human body? (10)

```
N C C M F R P Q Q A J Y E B A I B P Z N
C B V Q J E P V I Q A R O Z R P W X B H
C V M A G S A G W C B T N Q D X C F P L
L N U B Q P G N E T U M Y K E S Y S Y S
J D S R R I G G M A Z E B J S S B P N I
N U R C F R K D B V L G C A N G H E Z S
Z Q K O P A O Q S L A N S O J A P V X E
M E K B B T M H O E F O W W L D P J M H
G R E S U I Z W E S S U A I B Y L A U T
C R Y P T O G A M S U O S G E M O E J N
R R B X N N F M J F U C Z A Y T S G L Y
T U H U B B M E O Y X G E Z O I E X C S
G I D E A M G E A V R X I K O N M R X O
M V Q N P U H T O Q P E D T E V E X F T
U B B C E B V J D D Q T R T X N V Y H O
Z F I I V T Q J Y U Z O I P U P O M F H
D E N D R O L O G Y T C I D K H S T Z P
C R A A P I I U X T S R Y R U Q U W B F
A D J I I U P E L Z P P V N O R S K E I
D I C A C I B R O C S A J H P L V B K V
```

answer on page 120

1. What are seedless plants called? (10)

2. Energy is converted from sunlight and released by what? (11)

3. In which country the hormone gibberellin was discovered? (5)

4. What is the color of Carotene? (6)

5. Which plant has the lifespan of 4000 years? (6)

6. Which prevents the bleeding of gums? (12)

7. What science studies trees? (10)

8. Which living animal has the longest lifespan? (8)

9. What is the name of the process by which plants prepare their food? (14)

10. What science studies heredity and variation? (8)

69

```
B H E V C W T F K M H Y C M H N L O M M
E P X Z S A Z H M U X A F V V E D N I G
A P H V G I Q F A D B Q A U N D W A H L
N M R C O S A C S G I H Q R K P R W W C
I C Y E J F T S A W V R E Z Y Q C H L Y
U F P S W M W L T V Z F I R G P P P T G
O T T V W W E Q S S N W E N I H R A U L
T E S U R N E V Q A A L S A J O E Y E D
E J G X M D X Y E L A L Q O B G C S T M
B C G O G H X J B H N O P E N Y H C X R
N C F D M J G I W D A Y R O D L A X Q Y
O X V T T K C M L R Q T Z W R M M G O G
M O W Y D D R R T U H Z O V X O E O C U
U M R G A E Z A N O H A B L M K L E V S
S D T A P W B W O L M M N U S F E H F A
S M K S G U F K W H U M A N X P O W C Q
Y A P G V N E P I O V Q I H S O N E Y V
Z O F L R L A L Y E L Z F C P D V Y I H
H S F M U J P K D X Q K Z S C R U R V V
C H A R L E S D A R W I N H R U G Q Z D
```

answer on page 120

1. What is a flying fox? (3)

2. Which is the largest marsupial? (8)

3. Which the animal that has a tongue longer than its body? (9)

4. Who first discovered cells? (11)

5. Who wrote the book origin of species? (13)

6. Who introduced the term Physiology? (10)

7. Who founded the science of anatomy? (5)

8. Name the organelle where photosynthesis takes place? (11)

9. Who is the most recent and most highly evolved amongst organisms? (5)

10. Which animal has the biggest brain? (10)

```
L O F E S Y O T I F P N X U E V K K I K
A I N I F E H V D H B B R K L C E J R G
M U N O J Y L B X Y U C K V T I Y S O G
F J H J T H N U L I V S H J O A B D F Z
Q G M V C E Z Q R G A C A X T H O X Q F
X N W B T U B O G G X B F Q S C A Y W A
P L Y B O F Y O X P N X U A I V R X P N
W I Y A P C S N O R V R N B R P D M D N
N Z Z C U Q V J K W D P H A V O W D U
E W I N D O W S G M H S J E G M C R I G
M L I A M E Z I K O R T M R T H J F T Y
I U O K Q L Q N Y A J O W T J M D R C X
F N O N A C K Q Q G J N L C W Q O I G B
R D N V B V R G R E L Y C R B I G M J E
K W U C S C E L Q N M N Y M W H T X P M
M Z N W O I S H F W K J A D H O B T K W
S G Q X D B A B Q J G K V B F D I N E D
D Z F M I I L O U I S P A S T E U R X R
Q I N Y U C F A H Q C J L T O U B C T V
B Y L E M R B L F T R R G W M Y H V L C
```

answer on page 120

1. Who is called the father of modern biology? (9)

2. Who proposed the theory of Biogenesis? (12)

3. Which metal has the density is less than that of water? (6)

4. What is sometimes described as the "SMS of the internet?" (7)

5. Which company began as "Precision Optical Instruments Laboratory"? (5)

6. Which device allows the user to enter data by typing numbers and letters? (8)

7. What is a textbook-sized computer called? (8)

8. What is used for computer communication between users? (5)

9. Which operating system is made by Microsoft? (7)

10. Which beam is commonly used for optical data storage? (5)

```
N D Y R F C Y X X H R F D S T R I V V C
P S Q A J C B G Q R G X H I O I W L I G
U O M W C K B I D L A B I R A G I R O Z
B P H F X Y A H P O R R B O V T N A A O
T R Z S K T K Z L B K Z D N A L E C I A
M D E D O U Z Q Z O F L L G Y R Y B Y K
E H A H X T Q R D P E A B R D B C N B M
P T G M C E O N K H E H O E A L Y D W C
Q E V A T T F H N J Q A F E J Z O N B A
Y Y N S K N A R P X F M Q N C W H Z N S
Y P S L O T H H S V I J C C N K D T W Y
P Q V D T A I H T X L A S L N W C J S K
E U C Z E V O W F T J T O R G W D K P I
G E S U Q G S E U O E A W C B Z S F H L
K U L G G N Z M U M D R E X T O K Y O A
K O Q L P C P Y O G I W A L A C V O R K
G B T M E K C H W G K L Y G M O S E J I
O I Y L K C Q Q M A N Q B D R H L U I B
R T C B B I I S L A O O E U A A I I H E
A D V R U M F A V U V T V Q E Y M N N C
```

answer on page 121

1. Which color is used as the sign of conservation and environment? (5)

2. What is the transfer of electronic data called? (8)

3. Which is the city most affected by the air pollution in the world? (5)

4. Which is the world famous monument of India? (8)

5. What is the name of the program used to process digital images? (9)

6. What is the combination of smoke and industrial fog called? (4)

7. Which European country uses its subterranean thermal water? (7)

8. What is the slowest mammal? (5)

9. Which British Prime Minister worked as a research chemist? (16)

10. What is the name that links a national hero to a type of biscuit? (9)

```
A C H A R L E S L I N D B E R G H F J Q
Z M T C O L F S Q T Y O I S E V L X P B
T P A K Q G S T K G L B M C H M N N L N
X E W R C A J A S M G Y W K I O S F K Z
A L N H I N A Y J J W A Q R N L J R W V
S Q X Q A E G U F T E Y D L P W B W I K
T I E Z Q R C B I P N Y F H U O O O N B
Z V R J S B R U L K W P E H R K N C U I
J N R A J O S Y R O F U C Q H T Y Z W L
V D W H P W G L H I N W L P U L O U G L
V Q R Z X T L I T O E C N L G A G I O G
A Z D K W E J E V A U J H L N T L V Z A
S R P P R I N C E S S D I A N A A I F T
I J T Y L Z G Z S J J N I W N C J W Z E
F U G A Q J R N W F V X I N I E R Q J S
E B O F P J E Z U K I Y Z D I B Y P Y M
I C C U L O T R E B O D R A N R E B G W
P P M Q M F E A A U Q A D H Z P T E J Y
L G P M Q P Z L D P I O B I L R D E X Y
C F E K K L B Z C N N V J B P Y M X Q B
```

answer on page 121

1. Who was the Queen of Egypt? (9)

2. Who was the great woman who won the Nobel Prize twice? (10)

3. What is caused by the release of sulfur dioxide into the atmosphere? (8)

4. Who achieved the first solo Trans-Atlantic Flight? (16)

5. Who directed the movie "The Last Emperor"? (18)

6. Who was Prince Charles' wife? (13)

7. Who is the President and CEO of Microsoft Corporation? (9)

8. Who contributed most to the "escape acts" in Magic? (12)

9. Who was known as the "man of thousand faces"? (9)

10. Which city is known as the world of fashion? (5)

CrossWord & Search

#69

```
F V W A D F P W B P L D U J N A P A J N
A F A D C G F U I W S F T Z R O Y T Y S
S Z H N M I B T F H A W W I W H L N X M
N S N Q C T R M V H F W V I O U A N J Z
K U J E A Y O E B T M Z I Q N F I S T Y
K A U U J A F N M D I R L J F A W X V O
E C N A R F C S S A S O V I Y T F W B Z
C U O R N B Y Z O U H O T X C V F P Z E
W C Z S B N Z A R K R T T O M O G E U H
F K U D S F H L V N R E U G D T T G Z W
N U A C F A Q R A O M G A O M G N T Z F
Q G L W S O C A F B O N R M S M W U O H
I Q L Z G I L M O Z B T U A M M J X U N
R F S J X D O A Z W S R E O N C V F X A
H R U R L C B E R E T F X S O V J I E N
J A F L S F H U X Z S V R B E G I N A O
T H F I S M N L J X C C U R E R E L B Q
W D U G F N P R C L B B E K F R Q V L U
B O H I N F D T T C M U Z X G Z A K R E
L C G L T Q C M D S U X O Y L U N Q E G
```

answer on page 121

1. Kansai Yamamoto belongs to which country? (5)

2. Which is the place of birth of the fashion designer, Christian Dior? (9)

3. Where did large loose garment named "poncho" originate? (12)

4. Who was the first ornament designer of America? (19)

5. What type of hair ornament can be seen in fashion contests? (7)

6. What type of product is calico? (6)

7. The fashion designer, Coco Chanel belongs to which country? (6)

8. What is the type of wool cap called? (5)

9. What is called the capacity to do work? (6)

10. What is the name of the long outer clothing of the clergy? (7)

```
W I Y M J B P E D G F T W A S B C B S Q
F F M P T E A M E U G Q O O W H N B A U
F P M P E T Z R H R I X J M R Q M Q G B
L S K B G G R X D A E N I G I F L A T
V J S T U W J E E G U S S O N O S W T Y
T L I B L O W W H X Q T T O S G G R H W
O K Y X F L D C E T O O T M I M G T A S
W H O A T O E Q R P U E U L U F W D C F
S G A O P T Y W H A E L B O L Z T S H T
Y P K B F F Q E M B V A N T B U V U R O
D C I F F C R R L O B A K I L R K N I P
P F Q H C R F E E R R C T X T J Z S S X
U R O M E V U A B U I C T X Q R W L T W
H W D E Y M E B J S E X R W I M A D I S
Q G V Y A J S T S S I A I E S C W M E J
G E R S Q O X D T M Z A U S V H E H B A
M P I U A Y V D X T P S R Q D I N S L S
Y T M L Z N S S X W Y T B O O N L T P Q
Z H X D M A M E R I C A S N N W J O R H
V I V V Z M T W Z Y G O L O E A H C R A
```

answer on page 121

1. What is the name of the dress which is worn round the neck? (6)

2. Who was the religious reformer who started the Protestant Reformation? (12)

3. Which human bones, connected with head? (5)

4. In which field of human activity was Sir Mortimer Wheeler famous? (11)

5. What is the only woman known in the whole world for her detective stories? (14)

6. Who was the English leader of the Puritan Revolution? (14)

7. Who is the famous actor best known for the Superman movies? (16)

8. The fashion designer, Bill Blas belongs to which country? (7)

9. Who started fashion magazine? (12)

10. What is the name of hereditary dress of Indian Women? (5)

75

```
K Y H C L Q G Z T P Q N U W F T C P W Q
V F Y H W P V P N X U K P O L D V N W C
I O C A N O M J F E L E A K T Y G K G A
K T A O P Q Y R D I N W V O L D O L M A
L H I U D K H Q J G Z I H G L F L C A C
M W K U I D X L M H A Z L L X C A D L S
A B Z I I J A N O N E S Z R Z R R Q X T
Y O S J G K Q W R T I J G N D M V X H R
S B H A C O R U Q E G F A I N W A E D O
L S Z J M H F R F B V H G W Z E O Q L H
T Y U K J A U C C A U A Y F T K C H C S
U E M Z N F J O V R N O T R D L W A H S
S P A P Y S J Y G X U I O O Q Z B C S V
A Q J C H L H S P M F Q R Q S X U H W R
P B C G V O J F T M W N S I X T S P A F
A G A H C Y C E J R J S H Z L M B B T N
B A L G C A K Y T F F E A Q I X R W C W
B P R Z S H Q U T B O Y P Q W U G K H E
B Z U A C Q E Y I E V B R H E W O W S E
G P Z Y T J R W Y Q S Q V K S M S S U L
```

answer on page 121

1. What is the name of the loose covering for the shoulder? (5)

2. What is the name of the loose outer garment? (5)

3. What types of cells are found in lymphoid tissue? (11)

4. What is the name of the trousers reaching only to knees? (6)

5. What is the name of sleeping suit? (7)

6. What is the name of the sample piece of cloth? (6)

7. What is the name of cloth made of flax? (5)

8. In which country is Monte Carlo? (6)

9. What is the name of the knitted woolen jacket? (8)

10. What is the name for a Turkish dish made of stuffed vegetables? (5)

```
H D A P C S T R J T F V Q A J E X S Z A
K M I Y Q H M H A C G Y T T N T D P S M
U I D A A U W W J I R C R W U A Y Y J K
F N N T K C E M E W K K A R D D J E B A
D Z I C T Z M G B X G T K W A L Q D D L
D G N T A H D E G K A E E Q D E B C I R
U U Y Z E B N A Z P Y R C L W O K J J W
N P D I J D B I F E L W X B D V Z C Q B
D X A G Q O S A C R Z A V L K N E K D F
U W W S M G H T G I R B N H F D C K V K
U T J R S Y G G A E A R J T G N O K N G
K T Q Z N I L M H T A S U P Y A M V P W
A C Q B E W O F B V E D P X G L U V N N
C B F G G A I N D H L S Y A G N M S K G
E J D Z L G R G F O S F R P C E F D E I
K Y H G I Z G N N L Z O E Q Z E F B P M
R V B E G J W H D M O I M H A R B E S G
B U Z H E Z I K G G T W D I R G Y K A A
Y G X E E I X V V L Z Y E T M I A R R S
A M O N Z Z W F I L E R L R F V X J K S
```

answer on page 121

1. What gives peppers their heat? (9)

2. Which is the most ancient script of India? (6)

3. What is baba ganoush made of? (8)

4. What is the name of a loose dressing gown? (8)

5. What vegetable is usually used to make coleslaw? (7)

6. What is the world's largest producer of grapefruit? (12)

7. In what country would you find kebab as an everyday food? (6)

8. In which country did waterproof jacket find out? (9)

9. To what country is the mung bean native? (5)

10. From what plant does the granadilla fruit come? (13)

77

```
D P A I N J L X J Z C P P K E S E A X P
Y C M O E R P L K R Z U R F K R F W Z N
V H Q V M K T X H E G W A B J T I A D B
I Q J N E D P H O E P O N P G Y K D C F
I I E D Y I S T E G G S S C H W N Y J T
E Y M N O E E Q J I Y Q I C S R D O B X
G I M G N A T I L L H P C T O N E S T H
M P O O E K U F R C I O W C L T P S C M
J U G C I Q R P A F T O I T O P L O I U
S R H M W G M H B O S A T T Z G P A M Y
U C J P U N E H K I N E I U A H S X N R
B P W N X Q R V G T E G H S N P H V C D
P E G Q P A I Y H T N W D W U O A A S N
K H L B G Q C O I E C B I N A C C H I Z
M R U G D M N D F E W G F D S G R O C A
O T I S I Y N N O N X F R H F O I O C F
Q T K C E U L L Y H P O R O L H C F S B
C W W D Z M M J I M R N T R F W B D D E
B A E K K D X W G J C T R C A V I Y G D
E N F C F F H A D I R O L F A C L M N G
```

answer on page 122

1. In what country might you eat haggis? (8)

2. What is responsible for the green color of leafy vegetables? (11)

3. What country does the word "mocha" come from? (5)

4. What is the name of the cap which is worn by British statesman? (11)

5. What country is renowned for chocolate? (7)

6. What oil is used in the cooking of South India? (10)

7. What is the name of the flat wheat bread popular in northern India? (7)

8. What is the basic ingredient of curry? (8)

9. What is table sugar? (7)

10. In which U.S. state are the most oranges grown? (7)

```
Z M G L S B E B S J A C M M L P K A W E
P C R S K H P E X A B B Y H O T R W Q Z
X O W R J F T Q P X T M R J S K S C D F
D Q C R R G J E U J L L U O U S A A J D
P H H A A Z X X L X T R P N B A I Q W L
U B G S L G B S E T Z V A H L M D F D Q
G F X I C I G R K A W T S Y V J H F H A
M P D O A P F R Z D N H R A K X S V I O
A F Z O M V O O W N A O T V J A N C E G
Y N S E L K Q S R N X E R H M U C V L K
D G W R E H K N G N B A I A T Y L N U S
C E N T T O O H R F I V O M K Q J Z G D
K R E Z M F A B S D L A E T N I F Y Z U
V M Y Y U I A T V I G G D A J I Q L Q L
P A O P A D I R O L F D Q N G A M D C B
R N Z J G B S Z X V M E B Z K A P U R N
W Y Z D V F H Z O R I E N A J E D O I R
K B B K N D R Y P U J B P N I J E U E C
K H C A W O Y U D A E D T I M L W U F I
B O U S R I L A N K A B V A A A W T W U
```

answer on page 122

1. What is the name of the waterproof jacket worn over other dresses? (6)

2. From which island does cinnamon originally come? (8)

3. Which city in China has the largest population? (8)

4. In what country would you most likely find schnitzel on the menu? (7)

5. The Everglades in the USA is located in which place? (7)

6. What is the largest coastal city in Brazil? (12)

7. Mojave Desert is located in which place? (10)

8. Where is the Serengeti National Park located? (8)

9. What is the name of waterproof camel wool fabric? (6)

10. Which kind of tree does the spice called mace come from? (6)

79

```
L E D Z S Q N N A E C O C I T C R A I R
Z I E K N X O A D Z Z B J D R N C S B K
R R Z F K L L C P M W R L W H L Y S P O
B O B A Z C U B E A U P V E S P K P N Z
Z M P T R P Q J W Y J T W E W V Z Q Z R
T A Y R D B A W I S E X O B I O L O G Y
T N R Y L E M I E F M G D U D H S B O E
A I E P E L C V G S M J Y H C S P A L L
F A N L K C I C A W A M G T E C Z I Y Z
C W N R P D E Y S I P W C N A N O D I G
S D E U L E O N N C V G I U G D X U I Q
X Z S A P S H A K V E N C A Y R Y U D Q
C T M A E F M A M I N A O T W Q Y T J W
V R A E L S T O B E I N T A B B X Z B B
K S I V A Z F F P O A E D I L N Z M Y L
M L U T A I M A Q Y P P R K T V R Z Z P
U P D G W L E B R Q Q L N D C Z T L J O
D N M A N K Z Q X G I T A S N N D C W R
O S J Y B A Z C F B D B K P I P U M Z G
D E T U I S J F L O U G F U R L L V Y Y
```

answer on page 122

1. What is the name of the mountain range in which Andorra is located? (8)

2. Transylvania is located in which place? (7)

3. The George Town is located in which place? (6)

4. The Madeira and the Negro are of which country? (6)

5. The island groups called atolls are found in which country region? (8)

6. What is the mountain range of Italy called? (9)

7. What is the name of the state located in the southernmost part of Australia? (8)

8. Which is the famous country to make ornaments using ivory? (5)

9. What is the study of life in space called? (10)

10. What ocean surrounds the North Pole? (11)

```
F A N V N M A C X T E M P E R A T U R E
K G K J T U V O M P X F O O O T H T L D
C C D V C S A K V N L X K X J H J Y M K
U D V K G C J Q Q V S K M L X E C X X S
M Q G Z J A D A W C P C V M N N L Z P C
W M L U R T I V B O I O F S O S A K B B
P M S B N G A E S N N F I W A Y B U S J
B S F K B L Q H E D D M O C H G L J X D
B L B T T A Q A W E I E I Z F I P K C G
A Q P I O Y H H B N A R W S O D P B R I
W Y Z I P G N J G S F R S W I N P A D S
Q Z G S E M C N A A G A G Q V Q E I V W
X B Q P B X X M K T X S C Y D B X G U R
V I K K E Y S S N I D N Q G L U W W M M
G P S R F N F G W O D K R I R G O R Y W
U B C O I A U O C N D U D O Y P O B G Y
T F D C Y W B G G A T K G X M D E T M H
A O V N I L B X B B V G T B V D M O F J
T E T S U N A M I O O F X H I U R N P H
F I I C G Z R S K W T A A S I J U V S K
```

answer on page 122

1. On which island is the capital of Indonesia located? (4)

2. Which gas in the atmosphere absorbs ultraviolet rays? (5)

3. What is a very high ocean wave called? (7)

4. When a gas changes into a liquid it is called what? (12)

5. What is a low stratus cloud called? (3)

6. What is the most important element of climate? (11)

7. Where might one find the Acropolis? (6)

8. What is the capital of Oman? (6)

9. On which continent did our upright-walking ancestors originate? (6)

10. In which country were bananas first grown? (5)

81

```
P D A L S V S A S D C B U P N X K O D K
K E P F L Y A B V O P E W H V Y G B P J
F Y E E B H X H S T P H Q T S N C V K N
Z I U V A B E A B A F A L G V B Q R Q A
R Y R K R M T I I N Z T N Y C J T D A M
H A T U C B Q F G T N L H G Y S F C H D
C H K T H H G A A M R B C T A K P A S S
X P I I A W A H P E B Q V S A E A J I I
N P S L N A P D P V H B H Y I B A R D X
Q H S R D Y F D L B M U X V S H A Z X G
Y M K C R R E E B R T D N S P G U W B
B A N H B V H W A Y I A U Q U Z I S F P
D C M Z O E Z G P T R K E W R M Z A F I
F V T D N J Q M D R J R F I L D X V W E
U C J J N W K E M Y A Z O Q C A Y T S N
B I A X R O W L D W T N L S D O D D L V
J I I E Z X A W A E V T V B L K B O X F
R K H Q A G M L X E Y K N Z D R C S R L
D M L C I P E W F Y Z B O I O I J H H P
F E B S X D N A L S I R E T S A E P A B
```

answer on page 122

1. Where is the world's highest annual average rainfall? (6)

2. Where was the Bastille? (5)

3. What was the name of the supercontinent of 200 million years ago? (7)

4. What country has the most wild bears? (6)

5. What is a nickname for New York City? (8)

6. Which American state has the most interstate highway kilometers? (5)

7. What is the American state with the fewest counties? (8)

8. What is the chief port of Israel? (5)

9. Where can you see giant stone heads? (12)

10. What is the name of a crescent-shaped sand dune? (7)

```
S E F G U Y V Z Z W J L L W W U A D J B
N V F A U J R A W H D Z B X S P K N R F
H X E W R I N W S Y Z C O D N H Q F H T
V C N N W I L Z L P G L J S G T S X W G
G E G Y C D Q O L M Y H C Q Z I W Y L S
Q C L N A G R O A W H S S C J P M A T E
C N A Q S A L A F L W C P F I N P B U P
V E N T P U J Y L T M Q Z B X O B L Y I
X R D V I S O Y E C I I Y G C Y K B Q R
O O C N A T T T G L E M B T F O X D Y C
S L R P N R Y A N U Z L M A F B C F R D
N F V E S A B R A F V L L E E O E W W Q
I L E E E L B A F F A Z U B N T J T Q W
A A X Z A I W R G S F V S S I H I C U P
L H N A J A L A J E S U U R C O U I S V
A D Z T B V P T J J R U A T M I L J A K
S B G J E D P J K B K D X Z M I N O B J
K A E K R E H J L M I C T M L Z Y J G L
A J C Y B K E E M O C R P V D N N G I Y
Z X G C Q Z R I I A I D O B M A C B B O
```

answer on page 122

1. What natural wonder of the world is named after aviator Jimmy Angel? (10)

2. What is the highest mountain in Russia? (6)

3. What is Turkey's highest mountain? (6)

4. In what country might you find the Great Fence? (9)

5. Which state did the United States purchase from Russia? (6)

6. What is the largest lake in the world? (10)

7. Where is the Tonle Sap located? (8)

8. Where might one find the Ponte Vecchio? (8)

9. What science studies the structure and reproduction of cells? (11)

10. Where is Stonehenge located? (7)

CrossWord & Search

#79

```
C C Y J X G K N Q F E P K I Z L Z Q S U
P S N Y R W O K S Y L Y C I Z R S N V M
B I S X H J E I H D A L P K O M Y X M B
E A K K Z Z J O M U A W A S Y M D K B D
M L F A D A N A C O A J R N M Z N R X W
D U P O Y G E Y S E R X N D D Y E W W L
H Y X P Q V G J H G D E F R I Y X A S
I P T G N J J R O W E Z L F G F H P G T
X I I E B D W M I W T E B R L U A F D R
T B Q D M S G O P Z A O V X G W R E T M
C E Z C T X S O J Z H X R B Q F B T X T
E S S G B N I A W Z D L L X E B O L X H
O D P Q E N P S P X D D Z B Z H R G N G
E S R E T A T A F K T C K P B Y B C Y U
F J U A N R X Q P A T A B W R O R S W Q
N Q X H N I R S O C D N E V B R I W J N
R J S K Y W W L M N P A G H E Z D T R E
R P R E D U T I T A L Q M Y C S G D T T
O L J S K F B V U Y A L Z A G A E L B J
Q G V K G W V K W B Y W P K H Y I N R K
```

answer on page 123

1. What country calls itself Nippon? (5)

2. What is the largest steel arch bridge in the world? (18)

3. Where can Khone Falls be found? (4)

4. In what nation can the magnetic North Pole be found? (6)

5. What is the name of a hot desert covered with large rocks? (6)

6. What is the temperature at which air is completely saturated? (8)

7. What is the name of warm water that comes out of the underground? (6)

8. Which causes the difference of time between two places? (8)

9. What is the largest borough in New York City? (6)

10. What is the surface of the continental crust called? (4)

84

CrossWord & Search

#80

```
B F D J D T O S T S I G O L O E G R Q E
V F B O S J L Y L Q G H R W S V B Y O I
T G M C F K N R T Q V L X R N H F I E A
Q Y V Z A P C Z Q M A V E M D R V B P I
E Y O G S R R S A M L A P S K Y D E E W
Q T O H J W T E P G C P R E S S U R E Y
L L A C V O G O H M C S M Q D S P U Y V
B K D M G N N O G I S C G U R Q M R V S
U C Z B I U B K O R S V Z V F H P N B T
H I H P C L L Y J O A T Q Q Y K O U V M
K J P L X Q C F T C Y P O N B K M K T B
T T E V Z D Y V U G O N H R O C G Y J R
P U Y N F B R U E P Y J D Y Y O K L M U
S E B V D U M P T Q C T V O J B Z O M I
H Q I K C D Q F E P A D X O N C V G X C
L V X E F B N Y R T S Z J K A A U E R L
T S J D L Z U T C T H G N G C U R A E W
E V M L N M I P N L B R Q G L O Y X F Z
O E T G S X U X O K I Z E P X L Y R E B
S L K R D W Z T C O X U N L K I T U E Q
```

answer on page 123

1. What is the science of making maps called? (11)

2. What is the period before people learned to write called? (10)

3. Who studies about the rock in which fossils are found? (10)

4. The measure of Pascal is what? (8)

5. What is the term of the space without matter? (6)

6. Which human-invented material is used the most in the world? (8)

7. Aquamarine and emerald come from which gemstone? (5)

8. What can be classified as the Koppen System? (7)

9. Which company has a registered trademark of Ethernet? (5)

10. What is the largest organelle in a cell? (7)

```
G A H H G L D N U R O H B F V A L D G C
Y K H C C X P X A M I I P K O S A D B Q
R S A C U I R U C M Z F M C K C Z Q V P
E A N Y L A P O X N O I U H I J B L O B
N L C X Y N N P J U X R M A N K H J P E
D A A G R R Q S W Q X N M I N B K D V P
R F E R B S H J D G X A L M I F J F V B
A E N Q K H S O I H J O P S A N K L F P
G L B U L D T S F Q I N B R K O J Q M J
A V P G H A N J Y V V C Y Z W G R W P X
N I M U Q J C T M R R N S L T G Z Q R T
I S A V U Q B J B G R R L P S C K I L D
T P Y J O H A N N S T R A U S S X H T Z
R R K Z N M D E C I M U P O J H N W Q L
A E R U B A B K X D L L V K G M C R W W
M S L M U E U J G C K P L F N G U Y Z R
Z L K I Y T P A X Z T W W I W A T B S F
A E J W B A X T P G U F B T H N N P M Q
Y Y A G U Y M D Q D U F C N T D S M D U
N O B R A C A O K C U K A B Y U U Q B Q
```

answer on page 123

1. Which American state has the most earthquakes? (6)

2. What is the name of the floating rock? (6)

3. In which number system, there is no symbol for zero? (5)

4. Who wrote the classic "Logic Machines and Diagrams"? (14)

5. What orchestral instrument can play high notes? (6)

6. What country was reggae singer Bob Marley from? (7)

7. Who was the first rock-and-roll superstar? (12)

8. Who wrote Tales from the Vienna Woods? (13)

9. Where might one find a barchan? (5)

10. Which element's melting point is the highest? (6)

```
X R R V J Q E M R R R A B W Y J W M Y N
G G Q C W B Y A Z M O I F X E C K E Z U
X J K R C M T Q E U E L T O N J O H N W
A V J G M I A U C R R G V V B G H D Y K
S X U X U F M R U D V C A E N G L A N D
I U Q G J O T A J L O L C Y C L I N G U
P N M D S W M N L X B E P A V Z X N W F
P J N K X A U G U S T E C O M T E M T N
C O U F G I J U W J K L H J S R N R J Q
Z N Q M L Y N E W N L Q D G U P E U N R
P J W G K T V I Y O C V S H A B J S C E
G B K M Q V Z P I S Y W H B L X C E K X
U H P S L M F K E G K M K I D O T M Q I
X U Q Q G P A G X B K X H K T F E A Y E
F O U X Y L Y E E I D S L Z Y L M D H
M C A V B F C C B S I T A M D Y P G N F
A N I U Z B X L E V M N D P C X G W E N
X Y R E P R C X A J D Q D I O K I G O K
E H O Z H Q X D H M D J Z S J Z R O I M
A L Z P J T X X W X K E G W G O L B Q L
```

answer on page 123

1. Who is the founding father of the Formalist School of Mathematics? (12)

2. What is the oldest musical instrument in the world? (4)

3. What is the stage name of the rock singer Reg Dwight? (9)

4. What is the lead instrument in most rock 'n' roll bands? (6)

5. Where in the world was the first atomic power station built? (7)

6. What is the scripture of Islam religion? (5)

7. Who is the father of sociology? (12)

8. What sport take place in Velodrome? (7)

9. Where might one find a leaning tower? (4)

10. In which country was golf invented? (8)

CrossWord & Search

#83

```
H S I W Q F X C V D F X M O K O A D X T
W K Q K F C D W S C T J R C C C W H Z D
O R X N I T R O G E N S O X X L X C B U
N X B W U W A S H I N G T O N P U Y M B
L M L I B K S L C G F L L U I L F N E B
H Z M X X X C T O M F F G C J L P M T S
T O E L N R I J F Q D M R O U C U B M X
C W M T U S T E S U H C A S S A M A P
Y Q O A K F O S H A Y H G X B C N B Y C
I O S J X X I S O F V P E D R L T J K R
E K O B D Z B F Z W S Z V U X L K Q F K
L B M I D G I E P F A H F A S P O C K J
E I O O U E T D S E M N P V A T D L B I
C L R L E P N L M Y Q X T H J Y O B J A
T L H O G R A D C F O Q A Q S A Q X Y C
R I C G N D R O V Y K H R T S G I A H F
O A R I J E L F M H Y W Y F I P T A G O
N R R S V O U L G Q H S D I O C T T A M
S D Q T G S B P S X G W F H T O R O J D
V S M Y E A F F A S T R O N A U T I C S
```

answer on page 123

1. What is the name of the science of space travel? (12)

2. What is the main gas found in the air we breathe? (8)

3. What orbits the nucleus of an atom? (9)

4. What is the capital of the United States? (10)

5. What was the first sport to have a world championship? (9)

6. What is a person who studies biology called? (9)

7. Bacterial infections in humans can be treated with what? (11)

8. What is a single piece of helical DNA called? (10)

9. Which state did Edward Kennedy represent as a U.S. Senator? (13)

10. What is the name of the branch of biology that studies fungi? (8)

88

```
T W A P H N Z I W R X L K S Y T T T X J
D R B N D I Q I V P O Y H G P E T N F O
X W T O X S U Y V V W V K W R H N N J W
P L E T S I C I S Y H P D P B E C O L K
C Z Y R U X F K S G A V P J Z N Q S H S
A K S X E B K P M O R D G F K D J I O H
L A S O J H N E W Z E A L A N D I W I U
Q D R D V L P H T W E N Q J C L B Y U D
R F I E M B W S L I T H O S P H E R E U
C V I T O L S P O Q B H M M K I F W R N
O P H L S N F U P R D X Z V B A C S F W
V X D G A L X V M P D I L X D K H M Z I
I E E L B M K D E J C Y Q G N L S R H K
U V J Q E O E R E T A W H W M G U M X C
B N N Z U R O N H B Y H H K R A G M S E
F O Q Y I Y I S T K G J Q C E J A A B B
F C Z D D J P L V E T X O P G N W Y P X
Y A K F T E Z Z N S U C V L F N W J N S
U B O D A C O V A O Z N H F S C J Q Y H
X X X T B Y B H G R D T R E T E M M A M
```

answer on page 123

1. Electric current is measured using what device? (7)

2. A magnifying glass is what type of lens? (6)

3. What is a person who studies physics called? (9)

4. Which substance is made up of hydrogen and oxygen? (5)

5. What food is used as the base of guacamole? (7)

6. The kiwi is a flightless bird that lives in what country? (10)

7. What is the sweet substance made by bees? (5)

8. The wire inside an electric bulb is known as the what? (8)

9. What is the name of the water that surrounds the earth? (11)

10. What is the name of the rocky crust of the earth? (11)

CrossWord & Search

#85

```
B E H I O Z E W M R U G D Z N H A U C Q
H Y C E N T R A L P A R K P N N K K A E
K L I M O W B A S U D Z B O H X N S U K
K A D K A Z V A R E R J O M P C A R U W
D N J I S A J U W Z I M T F U J L P E N
E M B C L Y N S Q K Q S J K L U I F F L
B X V D P L T T F K R M M H D A R G V M
V H T S S Z X R N M E Y S O Y P S I R F
S W O O V P H A W E C W P C L N G X T D
A N E R Q J B L E Y Y Z I S N O D R N T
C Z J T R N Q I I H L N M K J M G Q L E
L I B A B C M A U V E W K F I W O I V J
Y O K X Q C J P B P K G A T L X A E S P
B A O L G D U X E J U M W M X Y R M I T
K N W E D F O Z N L Z K E M K E E L S B
V T A Y G A C S V X X T Y M S P H B K K
O P J S K D R Y V W S N T T E N U L W E
I F R A F L G N W P S G C R Q D M R R V
P S V D S D I T A C I O E O B R V V E G
M J L G O V O M H I P D C U Z M A G M A
```

answer on page 124

1. Earth is located in which galaxy? (8)

2. Dairy products are generally made from what common liquid? (4)

3. What do you call molten rock before it has erupted? (5)

4. What do you call molten rock after it erupted? (4)

5. The Great Barrier Reef is found off the coast of which country? (9)

6. The gemstone ruby is typically what color? (3)

7. What is the name of the highest mountain on earth? (7)

8. What is the name of the great park in New York City? (11)

9. Where is the Temple of the Tooth found? (8)

10. Someone who studies earthquakes is known as a what? (12)

```
G W V W G H N X S B W F M I K I Y O Q K
F O W B Q J F M T K X Q Y G W P X Y K R
S R B P O B L Y E G C L M R U M V C R R
L B E U H B H T A Y A M F U N U L N J T
T Q C V C A D Z N A R N G P Q P Q V Q R
U X R K E X B O E R F X O B R M O U R I
U N Q Q D I P J E E E T S Z S H Z S I U
K Z O E O H R D F X C C P I I Q R Q N D
D O J A O B I T P S J Y I M N R T N R X
E H K B N P F Z E A M A H Y W A A O I W
E L I O S C P H N R C I H M E L T I N G
P A O P J U D T T S R N W W U L I L Y D
S E V N I O K B K K X O K D A K B O E S
D A S U C P G J P M W G D T F S B C D T
N K D V A U Q K G H Z S I A L Y K A W M
I Y C I Y C N Z L T A T C L R E I C H L
W V Q F M F D X A N U Q S H O B T E U O
M X P K Z M T F I D Z U I H R I A M M N
N K Z V R R F A E L L E M S D D U L P T
H W J X T S I G O L O R O E T E M W U U
```

answer on page 124

1. The fear of what animal is known as "arachnophobia"? (6)

2. What country experiences the most tornadoes? (3)

3. What is the name of a scientist who studies weather? (13)

4. An anemometer is used to measure what? (9)

5. What is a dog's most powerful sense? (5)

6. What is the most popular dog breed in the USA? (17)

7. When a solid changes to a liquid it is called what? (7)

8. What state of the USA is the Grand Canyon located in? (7)

9. What is the most important factor for determining the climate of a place? (8)

10. What is the phobia of dogs called? (10)

91

CrossWord & Search

#87

```
V P J A D E H D T B C X X R J L U M G C
T G R E A T B A R R I E R R E E F E E G
A W A H Q X P F W D L U F D F A E V M G
K P A K A N S A X X D H I T U W Q W C S
G G V P O C F L O J P V U N O I R O N T
P J I R J Z X B E Q P V N Y G F K K X D
H I N B X Y F B Z P E S R N K K A F O B
I A W U R K N P Z T K Q K Y C E K T D N
Y N L R G D C Q N S V E S D C C K R L K
S W E G U Z A N E L C U M A C N R T O U
C H T G C R D B A E U C K D G A O B J C
C P H L L A A V E D V B L L A R Y Q M U
X I H N Y N X R C Q E E Q I I F W E R T
Z V T D U U G K O L J G D P Q O E I T W
Y X L K B D T K T R B Y D V W U N R W Z
Y N A M R E G N Z V S P R Y Y E I S I C
L A A B I Z O V A F L T X C O X N D L L
V J E I V N G Q O I F B Y L J L Q R S T
N K R K E Q B T Y K W J A J I H F Z I H
C N D R O D C Q S W O N T N B S S M A W
```

answer on page 124

1. What is the name of the world's largest reef system? (16)

2. What tree blossoming does the Japanese word sakura mean? (6)

3. What is the most common metal found on Earth? (4)

4. The Great Sphinx of Giza has the head of a human and the body of a what? (4)

5. Which country gave the Statue of Liberty to the USA as a gift? (6)

6. What country is Santorini in? (6)

7. Adidas and Volkswagen are companies from what country? (7)

8. In what country is the Great Pyramid of Giza found? (5)

9. Where is the Brooklyn Bridge located? (7)

10. When solids reach their melting points they become what? (7)

```
U Y J S K C O I N M O A Y Z K Q B F U J
M G D L S Q O A T B S P F K J T F V M O
A A M U F G B I V N A D K Q Y B O B N M
D L E R R G D I U X A D O G R Z S Y A V
C A J B M F H G U O P P A O V H W U A L
I T U P Q Z M V S S Q C A E R A U O L H
R Z Z J Y E C F V I E B B J V M C L Q W
C Q X H X T L O N L Z N T C I D A L H K
U Q O E L F G W A O G N A T X A F N B R
M O Q K Q J E Z N P G W A Z J L Y E N N
F O J F M B K S I O M L L X O S L X D K
E N L C T H N L M R Y L O J A X V S O Q
R G E Q S L N G E P H X W K Q J S R R P
E R U O L F W J Z Z L A U Z I K O S D Z
N X T R W C E O P W K H S G J L B F U Z
C O B E I M I G B V N F P X V B N V K S
E X B Q S W C O S C Q W O R U M P C F M
H E T E Q K M A N L H J U R M Q L R N W
F W I S T A N B U L U L S W X M G M Z K
Y S Y F X D X E X B U K D Q G N F H B T
```

answer on page 124

1. Leonardo da Vinci was born in what country? (5)

2. Mount Fuji is the highest mountain in what country? (5)

3. The perimeter of a circle is also known as what? (13)

4. What is the genre of cartoon art called? (5)

5. What dance is considered the most passionate? (5)

6. What is the name of a line that has no ends? (4)

7. What is bee glue called? (8)

8. What is the main ingredient needed to make pies? (5)

9. Where would one find the Topkapi Palace? (8)

10. Who is the first to meet a hotel visitor? (7)

93

```
T Z Q O Z S A N T T C W E M Y F B B Q V
D B A U W F D N K R S C G G C Y I L E Q
H E L J Z V K Y P T U E M X E D P K K D
I N F A L U I J I T J C D L V K E X N G
F E P R O M H C U I D N Z B R W I A B V
K L I R O M K R E M M A P S E O P A H I
S I E J E O J Y G P N L L U S T C H V R
O U P J K U X Y S O Y A L W E R U Z Q M
N V B L C Q P P D Z H B F S R T Q L A Z
E L B U E T R K C O L E P P O F Z B G W
M O S J H V H C J N E T G I D O H B P X
W D P T A O Y O V F R U J D Q U K J N T
Y U E E B S R E H P X L Z E E H Z V O U
S D N A L R E H T E N N E R N H P P N H
S L K H A J G D S D J V X W I K I T K M
G B I V A A Y C B I A H F E L E X X C Z
D N Z C R U Z J I Q B A X B R I E H G S
Y R O U Y T L P F M B P D X E W L V I W
R Q H O L N K Y C K H F F Y B U S W X E
A L H M M A L Y B V M P B A N D L Z D X
```

answer on page 124

1. What is monitor expansion measured in? (6)

2. Who is doing useless mailing on the Internet? (7)

3. What is the name of the main report of an accountant? (7)

4. What does a selenologist study? (4)

5. What is the main attribute of Charlie Chaplin? (5)

6. What is the name of the thinnest natural thread? (9)

7. What is the name of a large area where rare animals live? (7)

8. Where do the tallest men live? (11)

9. In what city would one find the Brandenburg Gate? (6)

10. What is the name of the animal with a hundred thorns? (8)

94

CrossWord & Search

#90

```
V Q I Q G L S Y L Z T A P L D T R Q C I
P Q L X Q I J M G Z B D O V Z D B J G P
W E D O K A J L N S N K M S E N Y Y H I
S Y W J U W H V L V D W B H V P F K Z L
H V T S W G M N S K J S L X I M M Y B O
M X S S M A N A P O A C H E R S I G R P
G N S L E X W H D I H G I B T V N H R K
U O U R C D E U S Z R X W K D F G J D L
K K T S H U U F V F T X L R C H D C E A
P S V D O G R O S E C N L U T V K Q Z H
W H I S B X K E X B A Q F Q S A I L W X
X S E I L Q X U A P S E Y A Z N G O X B
O L O L W E Q F A Y O O J N M U Z E G X
Y M T C F O N J I A H C P E E D R C N L
P O Y G I Z D Z D F U J K O A N Q F P C
R R U T R O I O Z O L Z R O Z A W X K S
F N I C K R L M Q G O E A B R L L T B U
Z I K C Q O V O H Y Q K U L C G R N S C
V N N R B R Z S G N G Y S K V N P A I E
A G B I I W G X L Y E L G F Q E A P E B
```

answer on page 124

1. What is the parent plant of roses? (8)

2. What is the longest living tree? (3)

3. What is the name of the small river? (6)

4. What is between night and day? (7)

5. What remains on the grass in the form of condensation? (3)

6. What are illegal hunters called? (8)

7. What does a boat need to keep sailing with the wind? (4)

8. Which is the youngest Social Science? (9)

9. Where is Hadrian's Wall? (7)

10. Which country has the longest suspension bridge in the world? (5)

95

```
M H I Y Q G E E H I J X G H T J C S G Y
V M A E W E L B L G F A T D X Z D S D X
S A X E T F Z C F I R G E G V K R T O F
O I A R V Z R I U D B H S R P E C X N R
Q C I T C R A K E U S O R C Z U D I P B
D P X O O T A N Y U D H M I W E V B F M
S Y N G K Z E L R G T H L W B O B A Z I
Y Q U N G R N B W U T I Q F O Q U D G A
D T D A Y U E A O W T T A S U N S U U I
L E A M R G K M B R X C Y E O O S X P L
L G O X A C R T E F B R O Y Y V R J U O
I B X S V E T F O C R P E H K B N C A U
N S D W V N T G U U B P S M G J J Z B V
U Y L I G V N P I J R L I G Z Z L W A R
H R R T L I B C H W S T J K H X L J O T
Z H D O M R A F E L V L G N E V M T G Y
X C V A K S Z N A V P F Q D D M A M A V
X C L I G H T N I N G D I F S U S A G K
T F O B Q P M Y S T M H X P Q J D W K B
X S L S D R X Q C U Z G C E G U X Q R P
```

answer on page 125

1. What is poured into the ground so that the fruits grow better? (10)

2. What is the name of the profession, the task of which is to care for plants? (8)

3. What is the most popular and most bitter herb in medical practice? (9)

4. What is a motorized sled called? (10)

5. What do Hindus decorate for the New Year? (9)

6. What is the name of the place where a river flows into another body of water? (10)

7. Which bird has the longest neck? (8)

8. What natural phenomenon can strike a tree and knock it down? (9)

9. What is the smallest ocean? (6)

10. What is the name of the line that divides the Earth in half? (7)

96

```
F Z C M Q E N E M O L Y W I Y V N A K G
C F K H G M X F V S Z V F A A U Y S H X
K K T T D A A F Q I M H Y L O A H X W E
U N D W H E E R P O G P T X F R Z B E D
L K C T C X N N Y V I M I J E U B O F V
O V T T T Z K L R P S K O B L K S F J Z
P A D I I S H Y L Z O G P V P A F Z R J
F R V T D T O G Q S V P D R E S F W A Q
V I L A D A M M A H U M P K A C X M Y H
M M S J I Y T P J J O K A I O L S M D K
T O C T U R B W S S Y V M J N N K U I S
E L K C Q M Y X Y M E H U D M S Z I M Q
C W D M M O I U F C C V S T D P G Y O M
W D M R M J Z D Q G G D L U O Z Y R E S
Y Q L K I P P G U I Q W O O N F C R R J
B A O W O L V N T H E X K N W Q J K R K
S C T C Q A H L Y M A R U E A A E T E J
G R Z D A Y V G W L G Q Z I L L U O I T
K I Y C Z I P O A X L I Z A R B D H P T
G V L G W C P P X Y E Q L A C R O S S E
```

answer on page 125

1. What is the national flower of Japan? (6)

2. What is the name of the person who started eBay? (13)

3. What animals raised Mowgli in The Jungle Book? (6)

4. What Disney movie did Julie Andrews make her debut in? (11)

5. What is Canada's national sport? (8)

6. Which boxer was known as "The Greatest" and "The People's Champion"? (11)

7. What is the only country that has taken part in all the World Cups? (6)

8. What sport is played on broomsticks in Harry Potter? (9)

9. Who is the king of birds? (5)

10. What restaurant's symbol is the clown? (9)

```
H H R X H M J P D U U E M T L T L C Y J
C Y M A E U H O N T X L P C G O R X S I
L F X F V I L G E O R G E M A R T I N K
Z Q H B I M M U N O X L V E U H T M M F
R W A Z C P X T H G E L Y R V E P O J R
K J A B T Q U F B Z I W R D V Z Q E I B
Y D Y I O S A M S U N G T M T T X D Q V
Z I P B R K X L G Y U E W Q F R U J L F
Y E F S I E D H P G L Y P J F M R U X D
M F B W A S U M A T O P O P P I H D Q A
H Q O L Y N H J C V I Y K L V M S F T I
S Z C U M X V V O K C C J K H S F I S B
I Z S E R O V I B R E H X U R M P P Y M
F Q I N D M I I H A M N P F T T G F S O
Y O S R Y Q Y U B C Z M C D N J X R X L
L Q X S E A I Q T J U J L M U A Q T B O
L O Z J K L S S T V F K X V N P L R K C
E E N I E S A E A C G Y I K H N H Z B H
J D N J V F A N C A V C H G S Y H R Y N
Y L K P W B F B D X G R I R X W L D X W
```

answer on page 125

1. What are animals that eat only plants called? (10)

2. What country is Shakira from? (8)

3. What river flows through Paris? (5)

4. What is the only country bordering the UK? (7)

5. Who wrote the Game of Thrones books? (12)

6. What animal is legally protected in Rome? (3)

7. Which mammal is known for having the most powerful bite in the world? (12)

8. Which sea creature has the ability to clone itself? (9)

9. What is the name of the largest technology company in South Korea? (7)

10. Which waterfall is the largest in the world? (8)

CrossWord & Search

#94

```
I I O S T L S S Y T U A Q M Y S C G X A
R S I V M D H N Q H N R L I G Y C F J Y
K Y L W U Y A Z H L A K W F T X V D B D
E K F S C M N X E X S D M D A J X N I Z
N J F B R E V O P X Z T O G Z H Y X P I
W I J E G L M Z T P E Q X O V M M G V A
E B G R A T R D O N W A I F E A T A C R
M C C G S U R A H T A L P H M S U S O S
Z J I O C C S R O M E G S S F I B Z A Z
V M Z J R I T T S C K C N E L P G T I A
H N A C I T A V R A H G L G F F V V G O
Y G G L T X P P C A Y A L O B O M K Y V
N Y G R R H U S C X L K R E G R P Q S R
G O O V L T D D S T J I Q E V E E Y B V
U W D U D W G E F G P S A A D W N L S T
D G G N O X O F T F R U U N X O Q Q Y B
N W Y H O Y A W R O N G S E N T Z B L L
P B D O P L Q N A O D T C Y F W W A Q B
M B A I L O E G A T Y P M L O E M H I Y
B V L P N Y Q C I K D S T B C B S G E Z
```

answer on page 125

1. Which continent is the smallest in the world? (9)

2. In which city is Tower Bridge located? (6)

3. In which country is the Brandenburg Gate located? (7)

4. What is the name of the tower that looks like it's falling? (11)

5. Where is the official residence of the Pope? (7)

6. What are words that are opposite in meaning called? (8)

7. What are words with the same meaning called? (8)

8. Which animal runs with its hind legs forward? (4)

9. Which country is the northernmost of all European countries? (6)

10. What is the name of a baby sheep? (4)

99

```
I T F R K R D X A E Y W L Q E E S A O E
L A C M T U N E C F E E P L T R N G R Q
B M Y E R W A J B W R R G O Y A I I V A
I P W T L X L U N M F N B F R C E O I H
C H O R G W G X F K A Y D N L K T G B H
P I U A W L N W C I A I H H H N O I Y Y
H B U U K B E D R X E O J F N J R I Y J
J I B S E W J T E G B I R C W J P B N B
G A P T N W C D X Q R D W I H K S G G R
D N M A A M K C P N U W S U N U G Y R W
Q S G E C J T Q N H G Q F O R F N M Z H
X D A C I O A W G T P N C L O N P G A P
R B Y M R Y V W A E B Z I K A Z N X E S
G E C W R H E U J W F G M D R G S E N R
R A V W U S B P B G I K K F K Q N H O G
J V B Q H L D W R M V U K I I Y J Y Z O
C E H K J M P A S R L K X N M F L R R A
X R S O T C G T K J A U E I G T F A I M
A I K F V D P O X Q X S D R S X U G T K
R F Q D H W L S F T E W W F I C R B G I
```

answer on page 125

1. What is the class of animals that can live both in water and on land called? (10)

2. What meat is not eaten by Muslims? (4)

3. What state in its outlines resembles a boot? (5)

4. What is a very strong wind called? (9)

5. What is a severe lack of food felt by a person? (6)

6. What are the nutrients required for the growth of an organism called? (8)

7. Which figure has three sides? (8)

8. What animal has teeth growing all the time? (6)

9. What country did David Beckham play for? (7)

10. Which animal builds a house on a river? (6)

```
R M S M R Y U G G Z D W T N F M X B G D
O N R N A U J K B N O F O F U N E E L T
O J T L X J B R A L F J P L X Z P F I A
K Q C P W G O L E P Z I V Z C X Z I N C
J U M C H F N A Z W X D D R K K K R D S
P C C N P I I P N K T H S B P A Z E Q S
D T U R F D T O M X W D I O D C K F H N
H P A D B V E D T M S Y A K O A L L G J
G J C U L S D F W V U C L F P P C I B K
K Z N L O O V K R F O B C O D L D E N V
Q M F G E R J T N R Y U A R G T K S B T
B E T L O P L X N S Y C B T I G E R A E
N K V V V O M F U B D R R G K Y E G E T
M E Q B N B S E G S O A C O E H Q B H R
Z Z I R O P U E U B I R T C T Q Z F C A
I U G G X S D F B R V E K D S A E U S M
D C H S H T P X Z E P P F R P U V I N F
W D M L J B G Y G F R O E P D S E E D Q
X W M K D B O T C D C R T M D G Q D L P
S Q I X E H C R P C W A Y M C C O P K E
```

answer on page 125

1. What is the name of the person who lives nearby? (8)

2. What insect gives honey? (3)

3. What is the name of the prickly garden berry bush? (10)

4. What device in the building quickly lifts people and loads? (8)

5. What is the name of the performance in which the characters only sing? (5)

6. What mineral is used to make plasticine? (4)

7. Which country is considered the most watery state in the world? (7)

8. Which insects recognize and find each other using light signals? (9)

9. What type of public transport is the "oldest"? (4)

10. What animal has not only striped fur, but also striped skin? (5)

```
C Z B W G C Y W U A P V Y O E C V X G U
P H S L H F Z L Z T Y E F U Z B S Y F A
Z M C A K X M C F G T U A Q P T P A G H
N G O P R W O F C I V Z H C L E G I X U
E L N P G G M L A N U G P X O T B W J Z
P C H N D Y F I X A O O S R J C L L S M
U U E R O H T R A D Z E A H Y O K X B E
L X N B V C Q Z N O Q D M T Z N L G I X
B S E H K R O N Z S D O B O A D T E P A
M O H S C A C W D G V F A T U C V U Q M
D Y G K L I W L Y N E A F A K U M A J O
V N Y G G R O Q R I B B H S O B N M I H
L N V S M T E H J K Z X T F A B U Q S H
Y N O W Q A E E N A Q U H O Q L H R H P
P I R T Y M E O Z B I B Y S J W T V R U
E A O F L C V O X N H K F S P T W Z N N
Y Y R E U E C Y N O L O G I S T Y C C M
Z B S I L H Z F U X S O K K A D P J H P
S Z E M S E G N R B Z D J Y N Q X M B K
J Y S T P A Q Q A Z B D X X Y L Z V I J
```

answer on page 126

1. Which bird has the loudest voice? (7)

2. What is the name of a society where women play a dominant role? (10)

3. What specialist studies dogs? (10)

4. What is the name of a poem that glorifies someone or something? (3)

5. What is the name of the carnival dance in Rio de Janeiro? (5)

6. What is the name of the literary love story? (5)

7. What is another word for sodium chloride? (4)

8. Which city is known as the City of Love? (5)

9. What animal is associated with ancient Egypt? (3)

10. What is another word for sodium bicarbonate? (10)

```
X R X V J P D Z W P D G U T Q M E Y T E
D K M U J P Q V B K H H I Q U E T E X L
J H V Y A O M C M F V X B F Z K A O L Y
R R M W A R L C X S F L S Z D S S D A O
Y S A I R G O H X U Q V L T R A H T K D
A V S B D Z C O S T M H H G C W J Z M N
B E Z N M T X N R Q P S J I F B V W Y A
U R S X X A Z G T L R I T T Z M S Q Y N
C P W J M I G D K C D C S D S D Q M R O
M V Q T W O B E K Q R Y N O N B S M L C
B S L Z E K U G L A C G I A T Y Z N L R
Q V W G Y N D A T L C C L F D Q X U O U
B J T X K Y D N J F A R A U H D D I U H
C E C C L A A W N V E N H O T O P B G T
D H D S N G M O I H D R A S H G Y O V R
G O I A B V W A T J G K A O O K K W Z A
L I C N F J R E R B G Q B T A O J D F L
B P L N A Y N N C R G O Z Z I N Z W Q I
T H G T U W Z T B A C I M O G U G X L G
M V T L E L T O B A K C D G T L G T E A
```

answer on page 126

1. Who named the Pacific Ocean? (8)

2. What is the most consumed drink in the world? (3)

3. In which country was ice cream invented? (5)

4. Who Invented Sherlock Holmes? (16)

5. Havana is the capital of which country? (4)

6. Which country has the most lakes? (6)

7. What instrument did John Lennon play in the Beatles? (6)

8. In which country did Gouda cheese originate? (11)

9. What animal is a symbol of fidelity? (3)

10. Which continent is crossed by all meridians? (10)

103

```
Z O Q C D O V F D V N Z W J N X P J X G
D E P Y G I M N J H E O Z G P L V J H E
C K L G Q K Y Q V R G O B V X G E J E Z
V T E Z F D X H S M T B V G D I X O R E
N I P R C J D I H H N M G T B T K F D G
P D R R H W H C U M E A L W X S A T Y D
U R D R L S T M A M O B V G K W T L G I
G R A A M W P I X A R Y Q M I C X Y C J
C J H G A U O R J N M J U W K W R H B T
W I I K U H I C A D L E Q H R T K K Y F
Z B E N N E V I S A E P K S A H T U Y D
M O S Q Z J Z V O R H M H D A Y F B J P
V C I N H K D Z G I L R R R R T X T X V
X Q H K E P T C S N I Y P R A A C S Y V
P O D F C A X S K J W W E Z N Q N Z O G
J H D Q G Q J O F A H B V P J P L O Z A
D Y R X W U H O V T E V I V C U F X T E
P L H L Y U K Y H U X B H Y M J X O U E
L X K B N B P V L V G P Z L Q J D T I X
V X K I O B F B V L R A K K U T W O J H
```

answer on page 126

1. Where did the accordion first appear? (6)

2. Which character became the husband of Princess Fiona? (5)

3. Who won the first Nobel Prize in Physics? (15)

4. What berry is the most useful for vision? (9)

5. What is the name of the tallest grass on earth? (6)

6. What fruit is similar to an orange, but smaller? (8)

7. What is the highest mountain in the UK? (8)

8. What is the national instrument of Ireland? (4)

9. Which bird is the symbol of wisdom? (3)

10. What is the name of a sign in music that denotes a sound of a certain pitch? (4)

```
S U X A L B H F S J I B P C W C G H E L
A O F I D J I U E N A F F J A L V R F E
Y M U P D Q T F N O S R H Y O U F D C O
O J L I L O J F D A T B K B I L A E N U
Q H A G L X N E F L R L E X Z Q Z N X O
R I V V W K A P B K O M U W A W V N Q S
K G M W A D I O V J L D A Q I X J Q W I
A H M K S D I S P X O I H S U C U V Q R
G T O E K V O Q M K G S I P H I E W J A
O I A M L B W T X W Y N H J U A D Y V P
Z D L S R A O G X X O E T G G F Y J H U
K E C F B M D T W L O Y T T R V A U R J
S D W E L S P N Y I D L E M U J E P P K
Z R Z A B T N L U K W A R T S G D P E D
N D C U T A N P H U F N A S D G X Q X Y
Y F X U C J S Y V A Z D L C U I Y O D E
Q U R I F L C P G L W H R F J Z L M A T
K V L H J V D P X J B O Y Y M V B M C N
Q E Y L E H W N T S I N O I T I R T U N
P M M I C K B N C N Y H M G Z S L S S M
```

1. What is the name of a complete calm at sea? (4)

2. What flower is depicted on the Buddha statue? (5)

3. Which sea is the most salty? (7)

4. When water comes to the shores, what is it called? (8)

5. What is the science that studies the stars called? (9)

6. What is the model of the earth called? (5)

7. Which specialist studies nutrition? (12)

8. What is the name of the famous California amusement park? (10)

9. Which bird has a leather bag under its beak? (7)

10. In which city was the first cinema opened? (5)

105

```
A K P F S D G Z L A O Z V H L I O K N G
G O B M O L O C D E T N T D Y Q M R E N
W B R Z X D V O U I O D P M F Y U N J L
N L U Y Z U R D I D M N Y D E N M A R K
Y L P M M F A D Y C A A G T V G H H N K
E X W G M G K H M B T L E S G T I N X Y
K Y P C L Z H V G E O L L G U A D K M L
N V Q R Q E U X C G M O W Y C T U L B X
W F W E D J T G M U A H W Y C H I R H I
I G N F Y V L U E A X H R V D H I S O G
K M O K V R X G U M E S F Z C G I L A D
X T A Q Q X P E A M F R L L N T X E E H
G F J H J K N P T U V M C O C A K X L R
P E V V L J P X S I U L J R E T Q N D Z
G F R Q K O O F S G I G D O S P B Q P M
G X R M L L C H A L E C Z L H J I M T S
J V I A A D A Z X E L L L Z X N T R M F
K P Y E N N M R V B B F H G Z A H P Y W
H N E Z Z C Y M F P V T N L T O W K G Y
D B M R J S E J G D F N S H N R G G V D
```

answer on page 126

1. Which country is the birthplace of the cuckoo clock? (7)

2. In which country was the saxophone invented? (7)

3. Which country does Easter Island belong to? (5)

4. Which city is the capital of Sri Lanka? (7)

5. In which country is the most popular transport bicycle? (7)

6. Which country's capital is located on the Nile River? (5)

7. What is another name for the Netherlands? (7)

8. What vegetable did the Italians call the "golden apple"? (6)

9. What turns black coffee into a cappuccino? (5)

10. Which country is the world leader in the production of cheese and wine? (6)

106

```
N F E Y U V A V U X B J J J D G L W A R
A U T S E S S O D V N T N A S S I O R C
S E M L O H K C O L R E H S H O P C S M
X P K S I O T E S N D X M O Q C I N T J
W M J V R S A K U S N M R R M I N X S K
G H U N B R E A K F A S T U Z X E Q N W
G A I D M M B G E C U L F D T E A S R I
J W C H I V V Z S Q R T Z P T M P P K O
R E E C M M F C V J Q A R V O N P M E D
P A R C M N Y D B B T X C B D X L H L I
E T L U C U H C L E X K A F O Z E A H N
V U Z F V W N P J B W W W N I L R H F E
T A Q G K W E H F Y P I L R I F J I B S
U G Q V D A V G K V X F G I S I O O I H
T F G E E N B D W L W D K I T K E G O E
V I G H I Y A Q X W B Y L Q P A H C S Q
V V B I T N Z L I Z I L N P Y P N Y E G
X R S Y K L D L G B L Z V T I X L Q N I
X T A U X V X I T N Y M U F C T K L V Q
D A L A S O T N A U E N V M C K F S X U
```

answer on page 126

1. In which country did vegetarians originate? (5)

2. Where does pudding come from? (7)

3. What is the name of the fruit that looks like a cone? (9)

4. What is the crescent-shaped puff pastry called? (9)

5. What important trace element is found in seafood? (6)

6. What is the name of a fresh vegetable dish? (5)

7. What is the morning meal called? (9)

8. What kitchen appliance is used to extract juice? (6)

9. Where did cocoa originate? (6)

10. To what literary character is the Baker Street Museum in London dedicated? (14)

Thank you for your recent purchase. *We hope you will love it!* If you can, would you consider posting an online review? This will help us continue to provide great products and help potential buyers make confident decisions.

Thank you in advance for your review and for being a preferred customer.

Bonus

Scan:

or Link: https://cutt.ly/cSYd9QQ

- US Letter print format.
- 12000+ words without repetition, 600+ puzzles.
- Complete answers for each puzzle.
- Hand-crafted and tested puzzles.

+ BONUS:
- 50 PDF Puzzles to download and print at home.

Solve puzzles!

amazon.com/author/brainstorm

#1

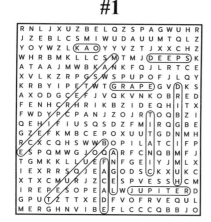

Hummingbird
Masterpiece
Facade
Jupiter
Titanic
Oak
Bouquet
Speed
Angel
Grape

#2

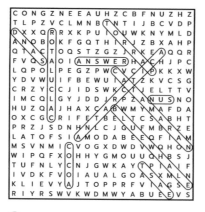

Cocoa
Catamaran
Answer
Calculator
Sun
Blue Whale
Antarctica
Sand
East
Parrot

#3

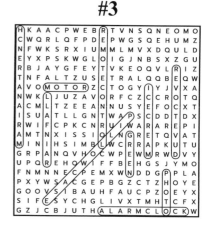

Mariana Trench
Ice Cream
Motor
Photo
Remote Control
Alarm Clock
Rainfall
Green
Duvet Cover
Pillowcase

#4

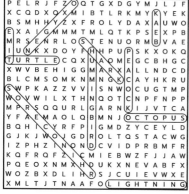

Oxygen
Lightning
Time
Beak
Octopus
Shark
Turtle
Hummingbird
Rhinoceros
Peacock

#5

Aquarium
Penguin
Shrek
Ariel
Walt Disney
Ice Age
Axiom
Sharp
Road Signs
Map

#6

Internet
Shampoo
Orange
Coffee Grinder
Refrigerator
Captain
Mowgli
Backpack
Ice
Anchor

#7

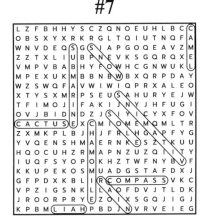

Vitamins
Camel
Chamomile
Cactus
Rain
Snow
Hail
Sole
Submarine
Compass

#8

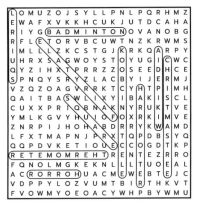

Squirrel
Square
Thermometer
Harry Potter
Badminton
Wikipedia
Fairy Tale
Horror
Christmas Tree
Electronic Book

#9

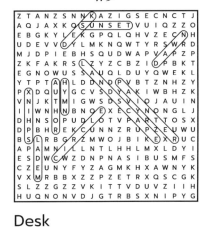

Desk
Sunset
Dawn
Medal
Landscape
Painter
Sphinx
Hymn
Circle
Author

#10

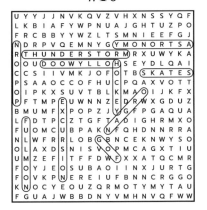

Skates
Full Moon
Hockey
Excursion
Thunderstorm
Fog
Popcorn
Astronomy
Hollywood
Organ

#11

Chameleon
Zebra
Botany
Zoology
Baobab
Ancient Greece
Pine
Nectar
Clown
Leap Year

#12

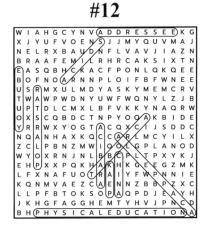

Physical Education
Polar Star
China
Youtube
Acappella
Arabica
Acids
Peak
Acrobat
Addressee

#13

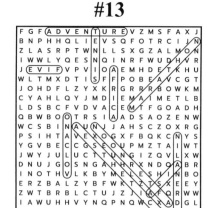

Adrenalin
Adventure
Aesthetics
Africa
Afternoon
Asia
Volcano
Tennis
Five
Marathon

#14

Albert Einstein
Ornithology
Earthquake
English
Uranium
Brazil
Sunday
Halloween
Greenland
Nile

#15

Peter Jackson
Katharine Hepburn
Keanu Reeves
Charles Babbage
Hotmail
Neutron
Weather
Oysters
New York
Karl Benz

#16

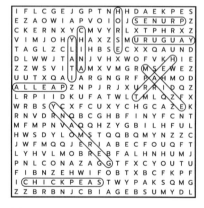

Horse
Uruguay
Maize
Prunes
Chickpeas
China
Paella
Germany
Italy
Heart

#17

Skin
Neurons
Calcium
Alaska
Vatican
Pyramids Of Giza
Sahara
Pharaohs
Cleopatra
Catholicism

#18

Olympus
Giraffe
Cheetah
Microsoft
Rolex
Football
Thanksgiving Day
Koala
Jazz
Horse Racing

#19

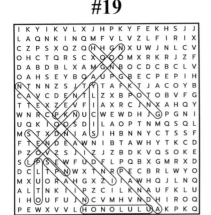

Spain
Indian Ocean
Pluto
Pentagon
London
Panda
Hong Kong
Seven
Sicily
Honolulu

#20

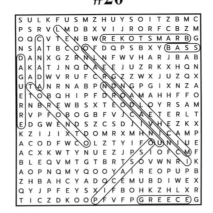

Toronto
Unicorn
Bass
Canada
Bram Stoker
Daguerre
Leonardo Da Vinci
Michelangelo
Greece
Picasso

#21

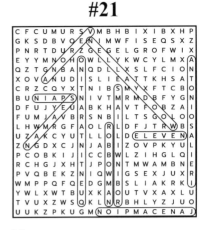

Verona
Eleven
Woody Allen
Quentin Tarantino
Rob Bowman
Robin Williams
Spain
Seaman
Jane Campion
Antonio Salieri

#22

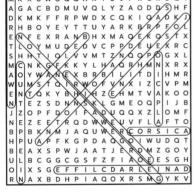

Al Pacino
Antonio Banderas
Daniel Radcliffe
Count Zeppelin
George Washington
Belfast
Josephine
Corsica
Erik De Rode
New Amsterdam

#23

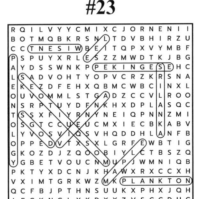

Sri Lanka
Pekingese
Paleontology
Mosquitoes
Wisent
Eel
Vienna
Dogs
Maple
Plankton

#24

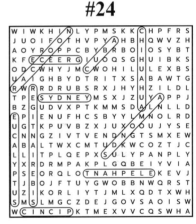

Siberian Tiger
Elephant
Raccoon
Chihuahua
Eucalyptus
Sydney
Almonds
Greece
Cuba
Picnic

#25

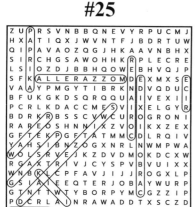

Mozzarella
Carbon Dioxide
Rice
Water
Paprika
Pisang
Coriander
Kiwi
Agave
Switzerland

#26

Dijon
Dutch
White House
Chrysanthemum
Blue
Penguins
Crocodile
Anaconda
Sequoia
Komodo Dragon

#27

Polar Bear
Gorilla
Tomato
Pumpkin
Maracuya
America
Condor
Carrot
Onion
Mango

#28

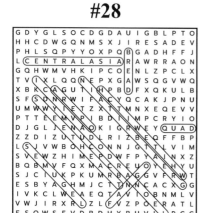

Legumes
White Witch
Opera
Bread
Central Asia
Fango
Quad
Sweetheart
Leonardo Da Vinci
Great Britain

#29

Cheese
George Washington
Eucalyptus
Fresco
Celtic
Ramadan
Kebab
Aloha
Gagarin
Blue

#30

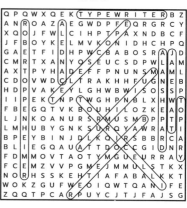

Telescope
Candela
Robert Oppenheimer
Torricelli
Alan Shepard
Topiary
Aluminium
Typewriter
Barometer
James Watt

#31

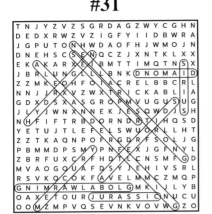

Alexander Fleming
Mercury
Diamond
Hydrogen
Sirius
Asteroids
Neil Armstrong
Reptiles
Jurassic
Global Warming

#32

Fifty
Enzo Ferrari
Sorbonne
Lion
Ganges
Pink
Cadillac
Mcdonalds
Mesozoic
Argus

#33

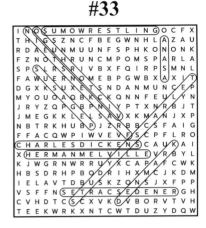

Pegasus
Charles Dickens
Denmark
Frankenstein
Rene Descartes
Study In Scarlet
Herman Melville
Sumo Wrestling
Asana
Victor Hugo

#34

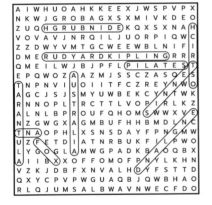

Tennis
Pilates
England
Rudyard Kipling
Fox
Ostrich
Tarantula
Ant
Edinburgh
Australia

#35

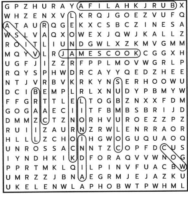

Cow
Brazil
India
Caterpillar
Columbus
Burj Khalifa
Visa
Leonard Kleinrock
Lion
James Cook

#36

USA
Robert Peary
Mercedes Benz
Steve Jobs
Forbes
Limousine
John Harvard
San Bernardino
Henry Ford
Australia

#37

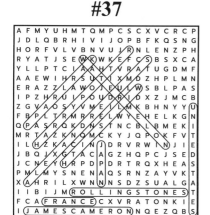

Japan
Alexandre Dumas
Karl Rapp
James Cameron
Will Smith
Harry Potter
Rolling Stones
United States
Watermelon
France

#38

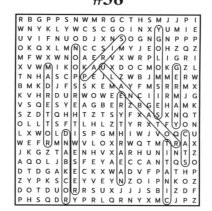

Paris
Seismology
Rock Band
Cats
Germany
Titanic
Reese Witherspoon
Ulan Bator
Rotterdam
Erythraean

#39

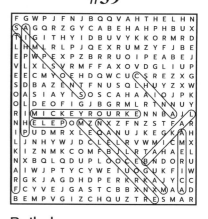

Baikal
Franklin Roosevelt
China
Simpsons
Melbourne
Pele
Mickey Rourke
Magellan
America
Philadelphia

#40

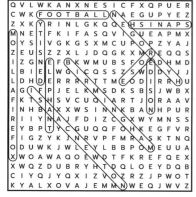

Football
Mozilla Firefox
Density
Rose
Isaac Newton
Edison
Hydrogen
Spanish
Elephant
Birmingham

#41

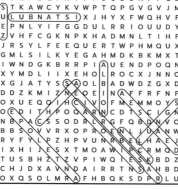

Raspberries
Lungs
Calories
Istanbul
Dead Sea
China
Antelope
Zeus
Neck
Albion

#42

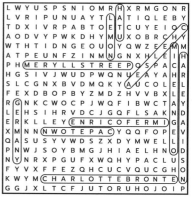

Lemon
Meryll Streep
Utah
Germany
Michelangelo
Chelsea
Enrico Fermi
Harley-Davidson
Cape Town
Charlotte Bronte

#43

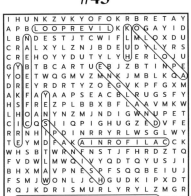

Manchester United
Liverpool
England
Yorkshire
Hulk
Coffee Bean
California
Spanish
Apollo
Walt Disney

#44

Yellow
Venus
Nike
Calligraphy
Tanzania
Microsoft
Mexico
Eyes
South Africa
Sweden

#45

Jaw
Colorado
Venezuela
Albany
Antarctica
Dublin
Rhode Island
Ottawa
Copenhagen
Nepal

#46

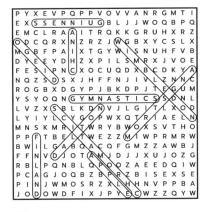

China
Guinness
Finland
Apple
Gymnastics
Diego
Wimbledon
Chromatics
Angstrom
Dalton

#47

Isaac Newton
Capitol
William Wordsworth
Vietnam
Mediterranean
New York
Eiffel Tower
Sir Allen Lane
Bacteria
Manhattan

#48

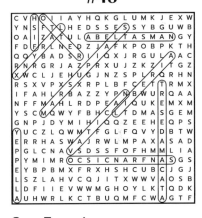

San Francisco
Otter
Marsupials
Larynx
Atacama Desert
Vatican
Liberia
Fish
Abel Tasman
Alleppey

#49

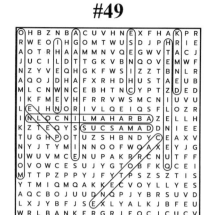

Abraham Lincoln
New Delhi
Damascus
Carotene
Pele
Agatha Christie
Chinese
Denmark
Queen Elizabeth
Mount Kilimanjaro

#50

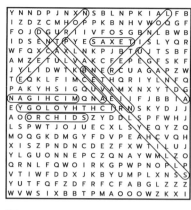

Plantain
Orchids
Retinol
Michigan
Ichthyology
Electron
Beverly Hills
Uganda
Texas
Auckland

#51

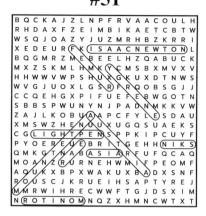

Isaac Newton
Mount Etna
Austria
Light Pen
Energy
Skin
Femur
Ear
Asia
Monitor

#52

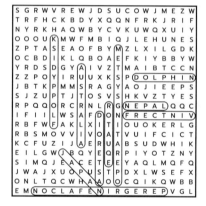

Equator
Floppy Disk
Asteroid
Peregrine Falcon
Japan
Vint Cerf
Operating System
Nepal
Australia
Dolphin

#53

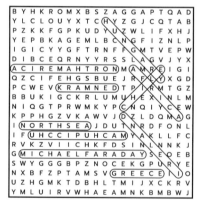

Ireland
North Sea
Chile
Machu Picchu
Michael Faraday
Africa
North America
Denmark
Greece
Hungary

#54

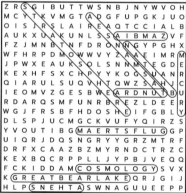

Great Bear Lake
Zambia
Mercury
Athens
Gulf Stream
Tasman Sea
Cosmology
Tundra
Stratosphere
Bhutan

#55

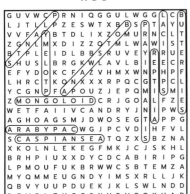

Caspian Sea
Botswana
Spherical
Ptolemy
Plants
Mongoloid
Praying Mantis
Butterflies
Capybara
Reptilia

#56

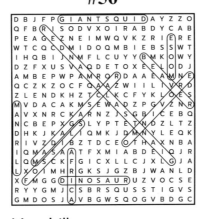

Mandrill
Moose
Omnivore
Giant Salamander
Giant Squid
Beaver
Dinosaur
Fossils
Africa
Madagascar

#57

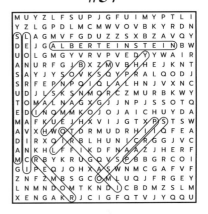

Bonsai
Picasso
Madame Tussauds
Romer
Origami
Leonardo Da Vinci
Albert Einstein
Paris
Humanism
Lithography

#58

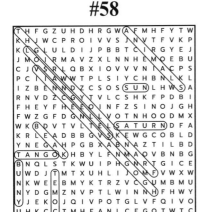

Beak
Sun
Frank Lloyd Wright
Vincent Van Gogh
Los Angeles
Bunny
Animals
Tango
Saturn
Comet

#59

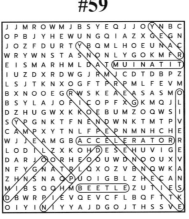

Titanium
Year
Ptolemy
Germany
Oliver Evans
Etienne Lenoir
Accelerator
Dingo
Dolphin
Beetle

#60

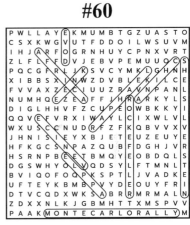

Knee
Monte Carlo Rally
Dove
Shel Silverstein
Rockefeller
Raphael
Apple
Venice
China
Africa

#61

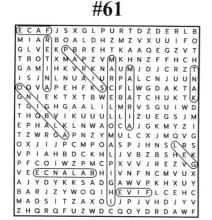

Paris
Leg
Malaria
Five
Retina
Balance
Albino
Marcello Malpighi
Kant
Face

#62

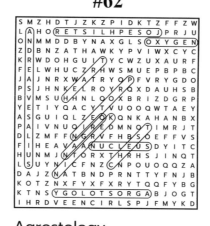

Agrostology
Oxygen
Chest
Joseph Lister
Organ
Nucleus
Heart
Keratin
Protein
Andreas Vesalius

#63

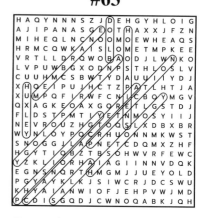

Cyanobacteria
Protection
Homosapiens
Blood
Atlas
Anthropology
Huxley
Histology
Membrane
Physiology

#64

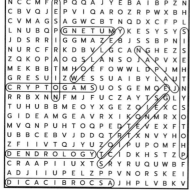

Cryptogams
Respiration
Japan
Yellow
Gnetum
Ascorbic Acid
Dendrology
Tortoise
Photosynthesis
Genetics

#65

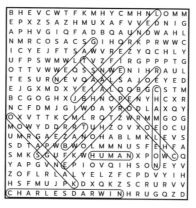

Bat
Kangaroo
Chameleon
Robert Hooke
Charles Darwin
Jean Fernel
Galen
Chloroplast
Human
Sperm Whale

#66

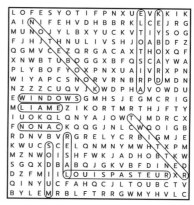

Aristotle
Louis Pasteur
Sodium
Twitter
Canon
Keyboard
Note Book
E-mail
Windows
Laser

#67

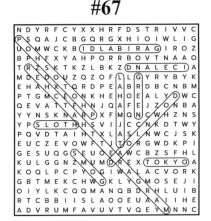

Green
Download
Tokyo
Taj Mahal
Photoshop
Smog
Iceland
Sloth
Margaret Thatcher
Garibaldi

#68

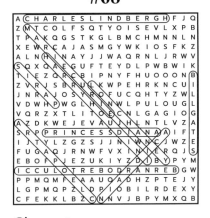

Cleopatra
Marie Curie
Acid Rain
Charles Lindbergh
Bernardo Bertolucci
Princess Diana
Bill Gates
Harry Houdini
Lon Chaney
Paris

#69

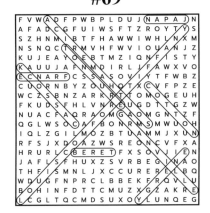

Japan
Granville
South America
Louis Comfort Tiffany
Tonsure
Cotton
France
Beret
Energy
Cassock

#70

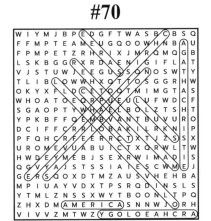

Cravat
Martin Luther
Skull
Archaeology
Agatha Christie
Oliver Cromwell
Christopher Reeve
America
Samuel Beeton
Saree

#71

Shawl
Cloak
Lymphocytes
Shorts
Pyjamas
Swatch
Linen
Monaco
Cardigan
Dolma

#72

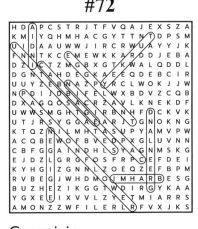

Capsaicin
Brahmi
Eggplant
Negligee
Cabbage
United States
Turkey
Greenland
India
Passion flower

#73

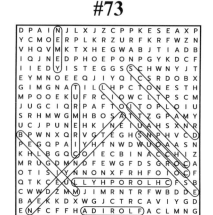

Scotland
Chlorophyll
Yemen
Anthony Eden
Belgium
Coconut Oil
Chapati
Turmeric
Sucrose
Florida

#74

Anorak
Sri Lanka
Shanghai
Germany
Florida
Rio De Janeiro
California
Tanzania
Camlet
Nutmeg

#75

Pyrennes
Romania
Penang
Brazil
Maldives
Apennines
Tasmania
Japan
Exobiology
Arctic Ocean

#76

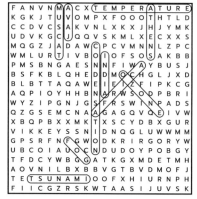

Java
Ozone
Tsunami
Condensation
Fog
Temperature
Athens
Muscat
Africa
India

#77

Hawaii
Paris
Pangaea
Russia
Big Apple
Texas
Delaware
Haifa
Easter Island
Barchan

#78

Angel Falls
Elbrus
Ararat
Australia
Alaska
Caspian Sea
Cambodia
Florence
Cell Biology
England

#79

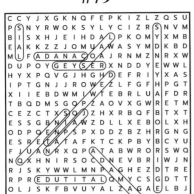

Japan
Sydney Harbor Bridge
Laos
Canada
Hamada
Dew Point
Geyser
Latitude
Queens
Sial

#80

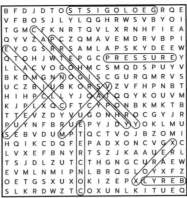

Cartography
Prehistory
Geologists
Pressure
Vacuum
Concrete
Beryl
Climate
Xerox
Nucleus

#81

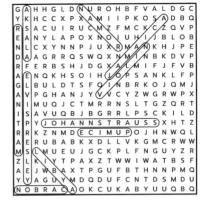

Alaska
Pumice
Roman
Martina Gardner
Violin
Jamaica
Elvis Presley
Johann Strauss
Libya
Carbon

#82

David Hilbert
Drum
Elton John
Guitar
England
Quran
Auguste Comte
Cycling
Pisa
Scotland

#83

Astronautics
Nitrogen
Electrons
Washington
Billiards
Biologist
Antibiotics
Chromosome
Massachusetts
Mycology

#84

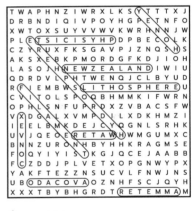

Ammeter
Convex
Physicist
Water
Avocado
New Zealand
Honey
Filament
Hydrosphere
Lithosphere

#85

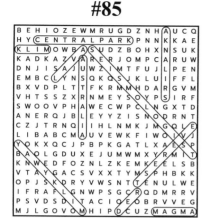

Milky Way
Milk
Magma
Lava
Australia
Red
Everest
Central Park
Sri Lanka
Seismologist

#86

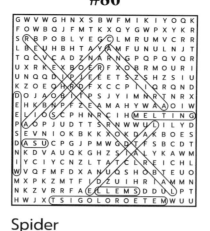

Spider
Usa
Meteorologist
Wind Speed
Smell
Labrador Retriever
Melting
Arizona
Latitude
Cynophobia

#87

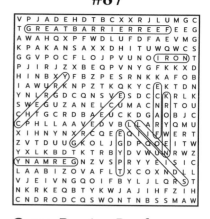

Great Barrier Reef
Cherry
Iron
Lion
France
Greece
Germany
Egypt
New York
Liquids

#88

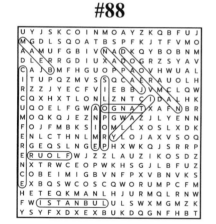

Italy
Japan
Circumference
Anime
Tango
Beam
Propolis
Flour
Istanbul
Doorman

#89

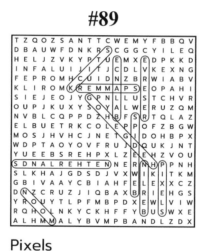

Pixels
Spammer
Balance
Moon
Stick
Spiderweb
Reserve
Netherlands
Berlin
Hedgehog

#90

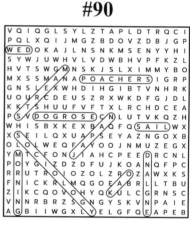

Dog-rose
Oak
Stream
Morning
Dew
Poachers
Sail
Sociology
England
Japan

#91

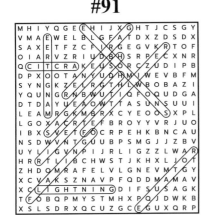

Fertilizer
Gardener
Sagebrush
Snowmobile
Mango Tree
River Mouth
Flamingo
Lightning
Arctic
Equator

#92

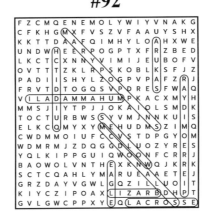

Sakura
Pierre Omidyar
Wolves
Mary Poppins
Lacrosse
Muhammad Ali
Brazil
Quidditch
Eagle
Mcdonalds

#93

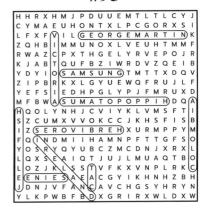

Herbivores
Colombia
Seine
Ireland
George Martin
Cat
Hippopotamus
Jellyfish
Samsung
Victoria

#94

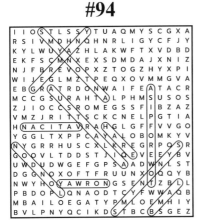

Australia
London
Germany
Tower Of Pisa
Vatican
Antonyms
Synonyms
Hare
Norway
Lamb

#95

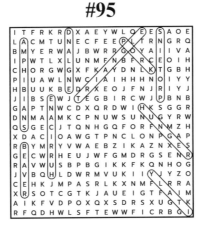

Amphibians
Pork
Italy
Hurricane
Hunger
Proteins
Triangle
Beaver
England
Beaver

#96

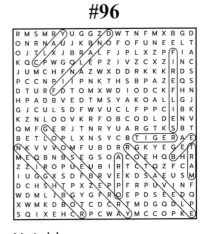

Neighbor
Bee
Gooseberry
Elevator
Opera
Clay
Finland
Fireflies
Tram
Tiger

#97

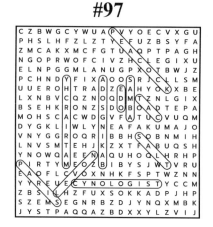

Peacock
Matriarchy
Cynologist
Ode
Samba
Novel
Salt
Paris
Cat
Baking soda

#98

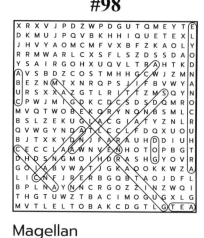

Magellan
Tea
China
Arthur Conan Doyle
Cuba
Canada
Guitar
Netherlands
Dog
Antarctica

#99

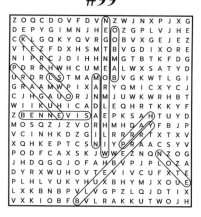

Prague
Shrek
Wilhelm Roentgen
Blueberry
Bamboo
Mandarin
Ben Nevis
Harp
Owl
Note

#100

Calm
Lotus
Dead Sea
High tide
Astrology
Globe
Nutritionist
Disneyland
Pelican
Paris

#101

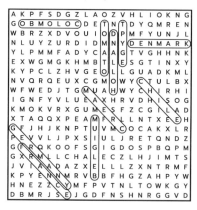

Germany
Belgium
Chile
Colombo
Denmark
Egypt
Holland
Tomato
Cream
France

#102

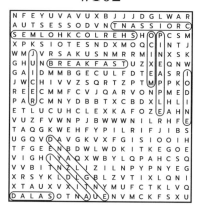

India
England
Pineapple
Croissant
Iodine
Salad
Breakfast
Juicer
Mexico
Sherlock Holmes